"Every diplomat and memb[...] should have 'Save Your Ammo' as required reading. It is a superb guide to understanding the importance of culture in all interactions and the need for the appreciation of culture in how it influences relationships, decision making, and policy development."

    – General Anthony C. Zinni, USMC, Retired

"Save Your Ammo is a must-read primer for anyone remotely serious about performing well in a cross-cultural environment. Easy to digest, it is chock full of insightful, practical advice backed up with real-world anecdotes that underscore the enduring concepts the authors' research has distilled."

    – Major General Mike Rothstein, USAF, Retired
      (former Air University Vice Commander)

"…the perfect guide for all of us who routinely are in touch with our world. It's a cultural 'how to' done through lively storytelling as we navigate global choppy waters."

    – Major General Spider Marks, Army, Retired

"Save Your Ammo helps readers … in one of the few contexts where cultural knowledge can, in fact, be the ultimate deciding factor between mission success or failure – or life and death."

    – Professor Emeritus Kenneth Cushner, Executive
      Director of the International Academy for Intercultural
      Research and author of *Intercultural Interactions: A*
      Practical Guide

"Among all the cross-cultural books that I have read (and written), the number, detail, and value of the stories in this book are unique. The authors are to be congratulated for providing such a valuable and actionable tool…"

— Professor Mansour Javidan, Director of the Najafi Global Mindset Institute, Thunderbird School of Global Management, and co-author of *Strategic Leadership Across Cultures*

"Save your Ammo is an incredibly riveting and indispensable book. Filled with countless stories of challenging cross-cultural encounters combined with practical advice that is extremely empowering, it's a must read for anyone working on international assignments."

— Professor Michele Gelfand, University of Maryland, author of *Rule Makers, Rule Breakers: Tight and Loose Cultures and the Secret Signals that Direct Our Lives*

"…an excellent description and guide…for anyone working across cultures in tense, ambiguous situations where split second decisions can mean the difference between life and death."

— Professor David Matsumoto, San Francisco State University, Director of Humintell, and editor of the *Handbook of Culture and Psychology*

Save Your Ammo

Working Across Cultures for National Security

Louise Rasmussen & Winston Sieck

Global Cognition

Global Cognition
1771 Southview Dr
Yellow Springs, OH 45387

www.globalcognition.org

Cover design by James T. Egan, www.bookflydesign.com
Formatting by Polgarus Studio, www.polgarusstudio.om

ISBN: 978-1-7334102-0-5 (paperback)
ISBN: 978-1-7334102-1-2 (ebook)

Library of Congress Control Number: 2019948028

CONTENTS

ACKNOWLEDGMENTS

This book would not exist if it weren't for the Soldiers, Sailors, Marines, Airmen, and civilians who shared their joys and challenges working overseas with us. We are immensely grateful for the time you took to speak with us, for your honesty, and patience putting up with all our questions. This is true whether your experiences were featured in the book or not. Sadly, we could not include all the experiences you told us about and keep the book a manageable length. Please know that even if you don't see your stories here, they were instrumental to the research. They form the base of evidence that the strategies included are best practice.

Ike Merrill and Ben Kennedy, we do want to give a distinct call-out to you to thank you not only for your continual readiness to support our projects, but also for taking the time to read an early draft of the manuscript and share your thoughts.

We want to give a big shout-out to Marc Hill of the Defense Language and National Security Education Office (DLNSEO). Our long-time friend, supporter, and steadfast ally in spreading the news that cultural competence isn't rocket science. It isn't a special talent to be nurtured in a chosen few. But instead a capability anyone can learn and benefit from. Marc, the good feelings that linger in the rooms you move through always inspire us.

Dave Rababy, a special thank you for all the advice, encouragement, and insights from your personal experiences you have shared with us through the years. We are tremendously grateful for your help making connections across operational cultural communities. Without those, we would not have found most of the other incredible folks who contributed to this book.

Jasmine Duran, our talented, dedicated, and wonderful research associate. Thank you for your piercingly thoughtful questions, analysis, and continued help to develop the concepts in this book. Your tireless persistence sifting through hundreds of hours of interviews does not go unnoticed. We hope that someday you'll again be able to read the back of a milk carton without looking for signs of cultural competence.

To all of you, thank you for your contributions and above all, thank you for your service and for the positive vibes you continue to spread in the world.

INTRODUCTION

Two *click clicks*. Chief Warrant Officer Duward Massey takes a deep breath. "The other Marine was standing behind me. I felt his back up against mine and I felt the safeties click off our weapons. We talked about it later. We both thought, 'This is it.'"

Massey describes the vision he had of his daughter watching the five o'clock news, seeing his body dragged through the streets. The image is still vivid in his mind, twenty years later. The storyline that could have been.

The incident happened on one of his first missions in Liberia. Massey's unit landed there soon after the civil war started. A small group of former Liberian military commanders had gone rogue and were leading mercenary units made up of children.

"These guys had names like General Sherriff, General Cobra, General Butt Naked," Massey recollects. "That was their names. It's almost like *Escape from New York* and *Stripes*. It would be comical if it wasn't so bloody serious."

Piecing together an operational picture was a challenge, to say the least. At the beginning of the civil war the gap in intelligence was tremendous. No one knew what the leadership of these mercenary groups was like. What were they influenced by? What did they want? What were their strengths?

"It was a pretty dire situation. A mortar round had just landed in the US embassy compound the day before we got there. There was really no other way to get information on these groups than to go out there," Massey explains.

Massey and one other Marine made the first journey out into the jungle to visit the rebel compound. It was two or three days after landing in Liberia. His last mission in Iraq had been completed twelve days earlier.

The two of them would be the first US Marines these rebels would see since the civil war started. They were mindful of this as their jeep plowed through rebel check points, five miles into the wilderness. When they reached the stronghold, they saw that it was an impressive fortress. By the looks of it, it could easily house three to five hundred fighters.

A rebel immediately ran upstairs to get the "General." "We stood back to back and we were quickly completely surrounded in this compound," Massey remembers. "There must have been three hundred of them."

Massey's voice tenses as he describes what happened next. "This kid, he was probably thirteen or fourteen, with an AK-47 bayonet strapped to his bandoleers. He walked up to me and looked me right in the face. His eyes were glazed over and yellow. He looked at me and looked at all my gear and said, 'Superpower.' He said it twice. Then he pulled out his bayonet and said, 'I am going to cut out your heart and eat it, so I can absorb all of your abilities.'"

Massey's mind raced. As crazy as the threat sounded, Massey took it very seriously. Although not certain, he knew it could be very real. He knew the rebels had a very different perspective.

"I knew that they don't think in a linear way—the way I think most people do. What made sense to them made no sense to us. For example, they would put on wedding dresses and run around among their enemy. They thought there was no way a bullet would kill a bride on her wedding day. Or they would paint their weapons florescent green with this crazy paint. Because they thought it would confuse the bullets so they wouldn't hit them.

"He believed in animism and that eating my heart would transfer my abilities to him," Massey explains matter-of-factly. Massey knew there was no way out. Both he and his colleague had kept tabs on their options for egress from the moment they had driven into the jungle. He knew that his only hope of managing the situation was through tact and clever decision making.

Almost in synchrony, both Marines clicked the safeties off their weapons. Massey had mere seconds to think of his next move. How could he get them out of this alive?

Moments after Massey clicked the safety off his M4, he brought the muzzle up a fraction. The M4 was now pointed at the adolescent rebel's midsection. The sunlight reflected off the blade of the rebel's bayonet. A drop of sweat rolled across his brow.

"An M4 is a short-barrel carbine. When I pulled it up like that"—Massey raises his hands and simulates a grip on an assault rifle—"I actually briefly touched him with the muzzle. If he had walked any closer, he would have walked into it.

"That was my threshold. If he got any closer, I was going to pull the trigger. Because at that point, he was at a distance where he could use his knife. So, I was literally watching his arms and watching his body. Waiting for him to make a move."

When he raised the muzzle slightly, hinting at a threat, Massey was drawing on his prior experiences. They were telling him that this simple motion wouldn't trigger a violent response.

"I touched him subtly, but he felt it. That, combined with my attitude, is what made him realize I wasn't going out without a fight. I think this is one of those times I played it exactly right to the razor's edge," he reflects.

"I know when it's simple school yard stuff. There's a bully. He is going to be a bully until somebody stands up to him, and it was kind of the same situation here. If I would have projected weakness or fear, that would have only emboldened him. What they understand is action. The weak get trampled, the weak get killed, and that's daily life there. So, you have to project strength; you can't project even the slightest whiff of being a victim."

But it's a fine line. Massey explains, "I think if I had disrespected him somehow—say, shoved him away, or if I had any kind of physical contact—that would have been dismissing him. Then he would have felt compelled to act and make good on that.

"So, I think I did the right thing and took it seriously. I think he saw in my eyes the determination. Through nonverbal communication I told him that I wasn't going to back down. And I think this also let him save face as well.

"I think this kid was trying to project amongst his peers that he was tough. He's thinking, here is the baddest guy in the room. Here is an American, I am going to go cut this guy's heart out and then everyone will respect me."

When Massey raised his weapon only slightly, he demonstrated to the rebel in front of him that he had power. But the motion was subtle, decreasing the likelihood that the surrounding rebels would see it. This gave the provoking rebel the opportunity to back off, while still projecting that he was in control.

Responding to the boy's threat, Massey whispered the only words he would utter in the whole encounter. "That wouldn't be a good idea." Massey and the rebel locked eyes. An excruciating silence ensued.

Then suddenly, the rebel laughed and said, "Ha-ha, OK," as he put the bayonet back into its sheath.

"At that point, when he brought the knife back up, that was another decision point. That fraction of a second, when I saw him move, before I realized he was putting it away. It would have been very easy to pull the trigger. And to be honest, I almost did pull the trigger."

What kept Massey from firing in that moment?

"It was the knowledge. The sure, certain knowledge that I would probably only get five to six rounds off before we would be swarmed. At that point, I wasn't worried about ruining any kind of potential working relationship with the 'Generals' or this rebel group. That wasn't even a thought. It was purely self-preservation at that point. Once we start shooting, it is really just a foregone conclusion."

As the rebel pulled back, he laughed it off. But Massey didn't smile. He didn't laugh. He didn't break character.

"I was just staring holes through him. And then after that, he relaxed a little bit." Finally, Massey breathed a voiceless sigh of relief.

After the tension unwound, the general's chief of staff came out of the fortress-like hut. In hindsight, it was only a suspiciously short moment later. At least, that's how it felt to Massey. The chief of staff motioned to the Marines to follow him and ordered the throng of rebel soldiers to disperse.

Working with foreigners is not just for diplomats. No matter what your role is in defending and furthering our national interests, chances are, you will work in some capacity with foreign people—people from a country other than your own—to get your job done. International partners. Local civilians and leaders, whose soil you're on. Third-country support workers. And potential adversaries.

You want to get the foreigners you work with to understand and respect where you're coming from. To get on the same wavelength about what needs to happen and why. And, most of the time, you want to create solutions that work for both of you.

But foreigners don't always think like you do. Their actions and decisions might not appear normal or even rational. They sometimes say, do, and want things that seem completely out of left field. Interacting with them and working with them can be a real challenge. There are consequences if you don't get it right, though. Potentially big ones. It's not just sharp words, but bullets that might fly.

To figure out what makes foreigners tick and find entry points for dealing with them productively, it's useful to learn some things about their cultural background. Their history, religion, politics, art, laws, customs, taboos. All the things that make them who they are. Studying those things can give you some pieces of the puzzle that can help you cope with strange, unexpected situations. Even dangerous ones that at first glance seem intractable, like the one Massey found himself in.

But here are the flies in the ointment. Unless you're taking a class, figuring out what to study up on can be overwhelming. There's so much information about culture out there.

You also have a lot of other stuff to worry about before you go overseas. Understanding what the job is you're going to be doing. Figuring out what's been going on before you arrive. Making sure your family is taken care of while you're gone.

Plus, when you finish up this next assignment, you might be headed to a new place. To Kyrgyzstan, Angola, the Philippines, or wherever. Then what? You start all over again?

The sheer magnitude of the effort can make you question whether the juice is worth the squeeze. Make you wonder if this culture stuff isn't just nice to have rather than essential. The relevance and value to what you'll be doing can slip to the left of your peripheral vision.

Here's the good news: There's an easier way to scale this mountain. It's called cultural competence.

Cultural competence is a set of skills that can help you

adapt quickly to new cultures and work effectively with diverse people. Once you start developing cultural competence, you'll discover that you don't have to know everything there is to know about a new culture in order to adjust and engage effectively. And you don't have to start from scratch each place you go either.

Cultural competence makes it easier to see what might be helpful to study, how you can use it, and why it's worth it. It can even help you figure out what to do when you go into a new place with a completely blank slate.

You can develop cultural competence by reading, studying, practicing using your knowledge, and building your experience working across cultures. But it doesn't have to take you a lifetime. You can get there quicker if you know where you're going. If you have a roadmap. That's what this book is designed to give you.

In *Save Your Ammo*, you'll learn about the most essential skills and best practices for building and employing cultural competence in a national-security context.

The advice in this book has been distilled from studies of more than two hundred seasoned professionals who have worked all over the world in support of our national security. These studies aimed to answer the following question: *What are the skills and strategies that highly experienced national-security professionals draw on to adapt quickly and work effectively in new cultures?*

The studies uncovered techniques that were used in practice by servicemembers who interacted extensively and successfully with foreign populations or partners as part of their jobs, like CWO Massey.

The research was unique in terms of who we approached and how we uncovered expertise. We defined a strict set of criteria for those participating in the studies. First, we wanted to make sure we were tapping into general skills that could apply anywhere.

Servicemembers who only have experience working in a single region or culture, say in Iraq or Afghanistan, might gain knowledge about working in those specific regions. But they would be less likely to have developed skills they could use across different cultures.

We needed subject matter experts (SMEs) who had experience adapting to multiple foreign cultures. So, we only interviewed personnel who had deployed or been assigned recently in at least two distinct regions and cultures.

The second criterion was that they must have worked with foreigners during their assignments on a regular basis. Sitting in a US installation or office, working mainly with other Americans, wouldn't be enough. The studies included people who had the chance to sharpen their cultural skills in the context of their jobs.

We refer to folks who meet these criteria as cross-cultural SMEs. Our study participants tended to exceed these requirements. For example, the cross-cultural SMEs in one study spent 8.2 years overseas in 6.6 unique countries, on average. Overall, participants tended to have worked in four or more different regions and spent close to a decade overseas all throughout the Middle East, Africa, Asia, South America, and Europe.

In addition to uncovering general cultural skills and strategies, we also wanted to make sure that the practices were used by professionals in all types of national-security roles. So, we included participants from very different national-security professions.

They came from all the military services, officers and enlisted members, and some were civilians who support national security. Foreign trainers and advisors, combat pilots, nuclear submarine captains, explosive ordnance disposal specialists, medics, special operators, convoy commanders, construction engineers, foreign-area officers, diplomats, interrogators, intelligence specialists, criminal investigative and homeland security agents, and United Nations coordinators, among others.

Again, all had extensive experience working with foreigners in various parts of the world for the better parts of their careers. By drawing on this diverse set of communities, we uncovered essential skills that are useful across national-security professions.

How did we uncover the skills and strategies?

Although we used multiple methods across studies, we primarily relied on one key technique. We sat down and listened to the SMEs. We asked them to tell us about their challenges working with foreign populations and partners. And they told us their stories. Stories about times where they had experienced uncertainty, misunderstandings, or had trouble getting on the same page with people.

But we didn't just leave it there. For example, a casual retelling of CWO Massey's story might just mention that he'd faced a child soldier in Liberia who called him Superpower and threatened to eat his heart. So, he clicked off his safety, raised his M4, and told the boy it wasn't a good idea. Although it can be gripping, casual storytelling doesn't go far enough to reveal an SME's thinking.

We needed to get deeper into their thought processes. To do that, we used a special interview approach known as *critical incident elicitation*. With this method, we would comb back through the initial stories that participants had relayed, revisiting crucial points several times over for a couple of hours.

Getting participants to describe in great detail how they handled tough intercultural interactions on the job gave us a window into their thinking. We elicited thorough descriptions of events, including the foreign person's behaviors, and the participant's in-the-moment assessments, decisions, goals, constraints, and considerations during the event.

Our next step was to sift through all this information to find the common threads. Were there commonalities in the ways these professionals worked with foreigners? Across these different assignments and situations that took place in various parts of the world?

We sorted through the particulars to identify the common skills and strategies they were using. Getting underneath the hood like that allowed us to start seeing general trends and themes. We tabulated and analyzed the results to make sure the findings reflected reliable patterns of expertise, rather than one-off anecdotes.

We found that a common set of skills were widely applied across ranks, services, and specialties. And across a wide range of situations and circumstances. For example, a Marine Corps Staff Sergeant might use the same thinking skill to locate shady individuals that an Army Major General uses to get support for a new government-run agency. They both take the perspective of the foreigners they work with to figure out how to proceed. The situations they find themselves in differ, but their underlying strategy is the same.

We also compared these seasoned professionals with novices, who had little to no experience working across cultures. This helped to make sure the practices were exclusively found among cross-cultural SMEs, and not the kinds of things just anyone would do. If the skills and strategies we had isolated were simply common sense, experience shouldn't matter. We should find that folks without cross-cultural experience used them. We didn't.

We organized the skills, principles, and strategies we identified into a framework of twelve cultural competencies. This model is called *Adaptive Readiness for Culture* (ARC). The ARC competencies help professionals like you deal with cultural challenges, no matter your job, mission, or area of responsibility. They are based on best practices, meaning they are practical, useful, and doable within the constraints of national-security work.

That's enough of our story. We won't go any further into the studies and analysis here. If you're interested in digging deeper into the science, have a look at our articles and technical reports, kept current on our website: www.globalcognition.org/publications

In the remainder of the book, we'll focus on bottom-line results—tips, tactics, and strategies that you can put to use immediately—along with selected stories and quotes to illustrate these principles from the pros who have been there and done it.

Each chapter in *Save Your Ammo* is dedicated to one of the ARC competencies. The "mission" competency gets two chapters. Your work begins and ends with your mission, and so does this book. Here's a glance at what's in each chapter:

Accomplish your mission by building relationships describes ways that cultural understanding and relationships help you do your job.

What makes you a strange stranger? shows how your view of the world is shaped by your personal background and culture and how to use that when working across cultures.

Working with foreigners through the good, bad, and beyond ugly offers techniques to manage your reactions and attitudes to work productively with members of other cultures.

A fun way to learn about new cultures teaches you how to take a proactive approach to learning about cultures, tailored to your interests.

Will your cultural knowledge survive a reality check? gives ideas about how to deal with bias in cultural information and build a more resilient cultural knowledge base.

How to learn more from your daily encounters shows how to further build your cultural skills and relationships by making time to reflect and seek feedback on experiences.

How to handle shocking behavior provides methods for making sense of puzzling situations or people.

Figuring out why people do what they do covers the tendency to oversimplify people and gives approaches to explain human behavior in more realistic and useful ways.

Get inside people's heads to gain trust, influence, and cooperation discusses why and how to consider the point of view of culturally different others.

Why you should engage others before you know enough shows how to break through uncertainty to engage with others and build relationships.

Ready, aim, talk covers the importance of preparing and planning your communications before engaging in challenging cross-cultural interactions.

How to adapt your style and stay true to yourself describes an intentional approach to your self-presentation to better achieve your aims in the culture and situation.

Back to your mission revisits the connection between your mission and culture, this time, addressing your influence on the culture.

The ARC competencies are organized to make each one easier to digest and acquire. In practice, the twelve competencies often work together, in concert. A single cultural interaction might require you to draw on several skills at once. Kind of like when a hockey player coordinates their skating stance and stick handling while at the same time using a teammate to separate themselves from an opponent.

As you read about each of the techniques, keep in mind that in application they are closely interwoven with other skills. And, when you think about how you might use them yourself, consider that it's possible to use several, all at the same time.

You may not agree with all the ways the professionals in this book handled the situations they found themselves in. Maybe you would have done things differently. There are many ways to apply the skills or implement the general strategies described in this book. If you can think of alternative ways to communicate, present yourself, or solve the problems in the situations these professionals faced, ask yourself this: Am I using the cultural competencies in my approach?

1

ACCOMPLISH YOUR MISSION
BY BUILDING RELATIONSHIPS

"If you're going to move freakin' three thousand pounds of C4, for the love of Christ, don't use Yahoo Messenger," says Marine Corps Sergeant Ben Kennedy.

Kennedy remembers the day he saw it. A bright purple Yahoo chat window on a screen in the Combat Operations Center. An Iraqi counterpart was click-clacking away. Typing a message about troop movements. Kennedy was horrified. His first instinct was to yell, scream, and raise a big stink. But where would that get him?

Kennedy had been assigned to a Military Training Team tasked with building up an Iraqi Army division intelligence section. His objective was to teach the Iraqis to run their own operations after the US pulled out.

"Me and fourteen other Americans were going to live with three thousand Iraqis for a year and train them," Kennedy says with amazement. The numbers were daunting and demoralizing. The intense exposure was weighing on everyone.

About two weeks in, the small team of Marines had a sit down. "They were like, 'Fuck it. I just want to go back to my bunk and go to sleep. I don't want to be with the Iraqis anymore,'" says Kennedy. The frustration was extreme. And, there was eleven and a half months left of the deployment.

Kennedy and another sergeant headed out for a walk around the base. "It was very creepy because we were the only Americans walking around," he remembers. "I had one pistol on my side at all times. Fifteen rounds plus one in the chamber. That's it. And there's three thousand Iraqis, so if someone wants to shoot me, I'm going to die."

Suddenly one of the Iraqi colonels came out of one of the compounds. He motioned for the two Marines to come in. Kennedy figured their situation couldn't get worse. So, they entered. Inside they found a group of Iraqis, including a general, watching soccer, drinking chai, and smoking. The general pointed to the teacups and pointed to the TV. Neither Marine spoke a word of Arabic, but they got the picture.

"So, we sat there, and we probably smoked three packs of cigarettes and went through maybe four cups of chai. I didn't sleep for like three days after that. There's so much sugar in it, it was horrible. It was diabetes in a freakin' cup."

Kennedy tried to communicate with the Iraqis using hand motions. But most of the time, they sat there in silence.

"We just sat there and watched soccer. At first it was awkward and then we did get kind of relaxed and put our legs up," he remembers.

This is when it dawned on Kennedy that getting to know the Iraqis could make his job easier. He immediately set some social objectives. And, after that he got into developing relationships full time, watching lots of soccer and lots of old American movies he'd seen a million times already. Segal. Schwarzenegger. Van Damme.

About four months in, the Iraqis started making fat jokes. Kennedy had packed on his usual winter "insulation" weight, as he calls it. He turned it right around on them.

"And there we were. Sitting there calling each other fat over hookah," he remembers, and grins. That was when he knew they had gotten close. "We were really having that relationship where I could be myself around them, and they could be themselves around me," he says.

This relationship became invaluable numerous times. Like when he saw the Iraqi team member using Yahoo to send classified information.

"The Iraqi Army didn't have a secure connectivity when they were first stood up. So, the American CIA made one for them. Only, they wouldn't use it. The way I found out why," Kennedy says with amusement, "is we were all watching *True Lies*. The one with Schwarzenegger where he's a spy. We were sitting around bullshitting. And that's when they said, 'The CIA is looking at us.'"

The Iraqis were convinced the CIA had put spyware inside the secure network to monitor their communications.

"They had watched so many movies about America and the CIA. In their minds, that's what Americans do. They spy on people and they're really good at it." Kennedy realized he needed to get them to start using the network without fear. But at the same time, he couldn't ruin their impression of the power and reach of the intelligence community.

"I came back and told them, 'Listen. I can't tell you guys how I know this, but I can tell you without a shadow of doubt that you're not being monitored. I promise.' Because of our relationship they had really started to trust me," Kennedy says. "And they eventually started using the secure network. When I left, they were using it full time."

Late night TV watching, chai drinking, cigarette smoking, shooting the breeze and telling awful jokes. All the heavy legwork Kennedy had done with the Iraqis up front paid off. That social groundwork gave him a different option for handling the Yahoo Messenger situation. An alternative to making demands or laying down the law. Getting to know his Iraqi counterparts gave Kennedy a diplomatic means to bring them on board—and in a way where they didn't just comply in the moment. They cooperated and changed their behavior longer term.

The relationships Kennedy built with the Iraqis helped him solve other problems, as well. For example, Kennedy never really felt comfortable using the interpreter who had been assigned to his unit in Iraq.

"The guy they gave us was an Israeli Jew. You can image how that turned out for us," he comments. Kennedy reckoned that working with an English-speaking Iraqi officer, Abadi, would be less antagonizing to the locals. Fortunately, because they'd formed a close relationship, he didn't hesitate to hit Abadi up any time of day or night.

"There were times when I needed to get something done, and I'd go wake Abadi up and say, 'I need your help real quick, man,' and he'd wake up, throw his clothes on and we'd go over and he'd be my interpreter."

The more people you know, the more options you have for who to work with. Make connections and expand your circle. You'll never know in advance who you'll hit it off with, and how the relationship might help you on the job. In general, the cross-cultural SMEs made time to bridge cultures and build bonds. And not just as a nice thing to do. They treated it as essential activity for job success.

You will get more cooperation if people like and trust you, whatever their cultural background. To get there, you need to find a connection and nurture the relationship.

Rapport and relationships with foreigners help you get things done. They can also help you stay safe. Army

Lieutenant Colonel Ike Merrill was able to sleep with both eyes closed in Afghanistan. He had built relationships that made this possible.

Merrill was one of only two American contractors serving as mentors at the Afghan Intelligence School. Even so, he felt pretty secure. Early in his assignment he met the general who was the G-2, chief of staff for intelligence in the Afghan Army. In very short time the two bonded, sharing pictures of their families and engaging in long discussions.

"He ensured that our vehicle drivers were special drivers," he says. Merrill knew those drivers were critical. So, he cemented his ability to trust them by making connections with them as well. "And I'll tell you what," Merrill says, "They saved our lives more times than you know."

One episode in particular stood out to him. "We were driving back one time and our driver suddenly made a sharp right turn up this alley. We were going, 'What the heck, what's going on?'"

The driver told them that a guy in a white Toyota Corolla had been following them. And that he thought he had a bomb. The driver alerted the security guys.

"There was a pickup truck parked in this cross alley and as soon as we went by, it blocked the Corolla. Another pickup truck pulled in behind it. So, they boxed this guy in. We kept on going."

He later found out that the Corolla was full of artillery rounds. The guy had indeed been trying to hit them. Merrill had taken the time to make connections and develop a trust that cut both ways. Making it easier to stay cool when the situation got sketchy.

"When you have rapport with people, then everything works," he contemplates.

Sometimes developing a professional relationship with a local or a partner can itself seem a little risky. What if they turn on you or take advantage of you? Plain, repeated everyday interactions, courtesies, exchanges of greetings, and small talk can all help you get a read on someone. Simple pleasantries can give you a reference point for what they're normally like, so you can spot when something's not right.

When Army Sergeant First Class Smith was a squad leader in Iraq, he found the practice of maintaining casual connections with the locals and his partners to be vital.

"If I have a relationship with someone, even if it's just where I can say, 'Hi,' and he responds back, then I have a baseline," Smith explains.

"If, all of the sudden, I come in the next day or somewhere down the road and he's acting hinky, or if I am getting something totally different—he is acting other than normal. Then my senses are going to be a little more in tune that something is going on here. That just helps me out in the job," says Smith.

Getting to know people, even just a little, might help you get ahead of a problem situation. Or, it might help you detect how committed they are to you or a task you've given them. So, how can you get to know people?

The cross-cultural SMEs routinely worked culture into their daily interactions to strengthen relationships. They used bits of knowledge about the local culture, history, or language to help them get closer to people and be better at their jobs.

For example, Captain Ryan Casper, an Army medic, used a few cultural nuggets to develop rapport and check people's attitudes. Casper has done two tours in Afghanistan.

"My feeling is, I don't want to get blown up," he says, deadpan. The tidbits of information he picked up from reading a little about the country's history helped him avoid that.

"When you're first meeting your interpreters, you have to figure out where they're coming from, what they believe. Can I trust him? Is he a suicide bomber?" The challenge was, Casper couldn't just ask, "Hey, are you Taliban?" or even talk about the Taliban in vague terms. "If you ask about the Taliban, you know that you're probably going to get a standard answer of some sort, 'Well they're bad, extremists.'" So, he had to get at it another way.

"You have to start a dialogue that gives you an opportunity to see where they stand and what they think.

You have to weasel your way into it somehow," Casper says.

This is where the tidbits came in. "I would throw some hints out there. You know, some nuggets of information that I would kind of refer to as call-your-bluff-type of information. Like, 'What do you think of Massoud?' I'd just throw it out there and see what happened." Casper then paid close attention to the response, the words and the body language. "I looked for indicators. Any reason to doubt," he says.

Ahmad Shah Massoud, the Lion of Panjshir, was an Afghan military and political leader during the resistance against the Soviet occupation in the 1980s. Casper had read about Massoud and knew that he had rejected the Taliban's strict interpretation of Islam.

If someone was for Massoud, they were likely against the Taliban. And vice versa. So, if his interpreter revealed any type of resentment or dislike at the mention of Massoud's name, Casper would have a data point about his leanings. Knowing something about the culture gave him something to talk about to develop rapport, as well as to get an initial gut feeling about loyalties.

"The way I see it," Casper says, "The more I know, the more I can roll in certain situations and test the water."

Marine Corps Intelligence Officer Neal Duckworth also came up with a clever way to use a bit of local language and humor to build rapport with locals, get assistance, and spot issues that needed attention. Duckworth spent nine months as a combat advisor with an Iraqi infantry unit. He lived, ate, and patrolled with Iraqi soldiers.

His command of Arabic was weak coming into the assignment, but over the nine months he picked up enough to communicate effectively at a very basic level. In particular, he set out to learn several handpicked expressions he thought were critical for getting by. They included the unusual phrase "*Shaku Maku? Wayn Irahabi?*" In the Iraqi Arabic dialect, it translates to "What's up? Where are the terrorists?"

Duckworth explains, "A white guy walking down the street with a whole bunch of Iraqis, and this white guy is going, 'Shaku Maku? They would laugh. Because obviously I am saying it like a kid. But then, sometimes, about once a week, someone would ask me to come in for tea. And I would take one of the Iraqi soldiers and they would tell the Iraqi what we needed to know."

For Duckworth, this phrase served two purposes. It was a way to interact with the population in a lighthearted way during foot patrols. It made the locals chuckle and smile. It reduced the tension. He also used the phrase as a way to take the temperature of the locals. To ferret out potential threats.

"You were able to identify those that wouldn't smile at you or wouldn't laugh. And then you could be like, 'Huh, what is his issue? Did we do something to his family?' So, I would ask the patrol leader, 'Who is the guy over there with the serious face? What is his story?'"

Duckworth would use this information to figure out who among the locals he needed more information about. Who he needed to work on and who he should watch his back around. "The people who aren't smiling, you always have to keep an eye on them," he explains.

Making connections and building relationships with foreigners can feel like volunteering for the low ground in an uphill battle. They look different. Talk different. Think different. Smell different.

It's easier to make friends with people who are just like you. Yet, building professional relationships isn't just about making friends. You may not know how ahead of time, but somewhere along the way the relationships you build will help support your mission.

Stretch yourself a little and connect with someone. In the words of Army Ranger Colonel Scott Waterman, "Don't just spend another day wishing you were home."

To start, set some simple goals to reach out and connect. Look for something you have in common: likes, dislikes, habits, hobbies, values, opinions. Maybe it's as light as tattoos or local sports. When you find that something, capitalize on it and talk about it to begin building rapport. This will help you start forming the relationships critical to your job.

Then, pull something you know about their culture into the conversation and take the relationship a bit further. Set objectives to find out a little more about the people you'll work with. Some funny phrases in their language, a person or historical event they might think favorably of, or not.

Finding people you connect with can make your time overseas a little more pleasant. And, it can help you stay safer and get your work done.

Key Points

- Building relationships across cultures helps you do your job

- Set social objectives that support your mission objectives

- Use information about the culture to boost relationships and achieve your goals

2

WHAT MAKES YOU A STRANGE STRANGER?

"I hit a motorcyclist. It wasn't my fault," says Army Lieutenant Colonel Reyes, drawing in a deep breath. "I was really in shock, you know. I didn't know what to do. That was the first accident I've been in. I'd never been in an accident, even here in the States."

The accident itself was traumatic enough. The mental gymnastics Reyes had to do afterward to control her instinctual reaction really took it out of her.

Reyes was driving her Japanese language instructor from the base across town to see another student. It was dark, and streetlights and traffic lights reflected brightly off the wet pavement.

"I thought it was a green light for me. Apparently, it wasn't, because I was making a turn. And *that* light was red. So, I hit an oncoming motorcyclist."

The minutes that followed are a bit of a blur. Reyes remembers the young man lying in the road. People quickly gathered and it seemed like the local police were there in a flash. Reyes and the instructor had only made it a mile out from the base, so the military police had also rushed to the scene. An ambulance came and went.

The next thing Reyes knew she was sitting in an interrogation room at the local police station explaining what had happened. She was released and asked to come back a few days later. Shortly after, Reyes's commander simply told her to "take care of it," so it wouldn't have to go on her blotter.

The next day, she got a call from an agent from her insurance company. His recommendation took her aback.

"He asked me if I had seen the man's family. I said, 'Oh, no. I haven't seen them.' Then he said, 'You need to. I would recommend that you go and see them. See how he's doing and apologize.'"

Reyes was in disbelief. Her first reaction was immediate and strong. Objection. She didn't want to do it. It was like a great invisible force was pulling her in the other direction. All she could think about was ways to get out of this without apologizing. It felt wrong.

Conflicted and confused, she ran the recommendation by her Japanese instructor. She agreed with the insurance agent. It would be in Reyes's best interest to visit the family and apologize. Reyes saw that there was no way out of it. All the signs pointed in the same direction. Still, why was it so hard for her?

She could have just pressed on, followed her intuition, listened to that part of her brain telling her what was normal. But she didn't. She looked inward and thought about her own background and culture. She asked herself, "What is it about me that makes this so difficult?"

She then realized it ran against everything she knew about how you should behave in this kind of situation.

"In the US, that's rule number one in an accident, right? Never admit that you're at fault. Because if you do, then you get sued. And to have the insurance guy tell me to apologize. It would be unheard of. It was so hard because it ran counter to my beliefs," she says.

Reyes realized that she wasn't used to the idea of apologizing after an accident.

"It was my fault," she says. "But the American mentality of "Wait a minute, you can't say it's your fault" was so strong. I had to just kind of go, 'OK, you're not in the States anymore. You're in Japan, so do it the way they do things over here.'"

Reyes discovered that Japanese people have different ideas about responsibility and restitution. Apologizing in Japan wouldn't have the same meaning or consequences as it would in the US. So, she did it.

Reyes studied up and practiced a formal Japanese apology. She brought sake and flowers to the family's house. They offered her tea and she apologized. She visited with the young man, who had been hospitalized for a couple of days but was now back home. She made some small talk about what she was doing in Japan. She told them she'd never hit anyone on a motorcycle before.

"The family was very nice. They were very, very understanding of me. I'd been expecting they'd want to sue me for hitting the boy."

A few weeks later in court, the judge asked Reyes if she had seen the family. She told him about the visit, and the judge nodded approvingly. There were no further sanctions or punishment. She is convinced she would have been worse off if she hadn't made amends to the family.

"It could have affected my career," she says. "Luckily it didn't. I think that's a Japanese mentality, as far as the culture. As long as you apologize, you take responsibility, and that's what people accept. Just own up to your mistake and things will be OK."

Going into a new culture can be disorienting. At first everything can seem completely strange. Then later you notice the things that are pretty much the same as back home. After a while you realize, no, things really are different. Similarities and differences float in and out of focus. It can feel like you've stepped into an eddy with a strong undertow.

You can't avoid culture by just staying clear of the restaurants, the movie theaters, or cultural events like national holiday celebrations. Culture crops up everywhere in the things people say and do and expect. When you speak softly, they keep yelling. When you try to plan, they just want to skip to execution. You're worried about a lawsuit; they expect an apology.

Unfortunately, there's no quick fix, no Dramamine-equivalent for culture dizziness. Because culture is not a disease. It's normal. We all have one, including you. No matter where you are now, no matter where you grew up: You have a culture.

When you see or hear something, your mind attaches a label to it. It's good, bad, flattering, insulting. Your background, history, and culture colors your perception, whether you want it to or not. It happens automatically, and it happens fast.

"Oh my god! Look at them!" Army Sergeant First Class Jean Hightower puts her hands over her eyes and simulates shock. Hightower attended interrogators' school in Munich, Germany. She and a group of fellow students decided to go on a rafting trip on the Isar river. It turned out to be an eye-opening day on the water.

"I was born in Boston. But when I was a kid, we moved to this little suburb that had six thousand people in it, and that was really pretty much all I knew. That's how I grew up. In little suburbia, where everybody is pretty much the same." Hightower was in Munich in the springtime. It was getting warm outside. Blankets were placed on grass. Books and toys and games had come out. And bikini tops had come off.

"We all just kind of looked at each other like, 'Oh my god!'" Hightower's first thought? It was shocking. Scandalous. She reflects for a moment and continues. "Afterward I thought about it, and it kind of dawned on me that it was OK. Or at least 'there' it was OK. I started thinking that maybe my way of looking at it, maybe I'm just too repressed about this kind of thing. Maybe I need to open my eyes, or open my outlook. Woo-hoo, it's OK."

After a while Hightower accepted the public nudity phenomenon. So much so that she started wondering why Americans are so inhibited about it in the first place.

"They show more nudity on TV over there too," she says. "And we just won't do that because there's something wrong with the human body, I guess. We are supposed to be the best country to live in. The strongest, the most powerful, the richest, and all that. But we're also one of the most repressed in some respects." Hightower did a 180 in her thinking.

You don't have to start going topless. Or wear speedos. Adopting another culture's ways of thinking and behaving doesn't have to be your goal. Yet, you can save some time trying to understand other cultures by being a little more aware of your own culture.

Doing so can help you spot real, fundamental differences in the ways different groups solve their problems. And see past immorality, disrespect, slights, and insults where maybe they don't exist—this will make your dealings with people from the other culture a tad less stressful.

Take this example. Drivers in some other cultures lay on their horns. All the time. It's rude, right?

"It's kind of insane how many times you hear a horn beep over there in a day," says Staff Sergeant Dixon. He worked in Cambodia for three months building a school. Every day he spent about a half hour in a car each way from his accommodations to his job site.

The cacophony of car horns was earsplitting. Every morning the sound of it made Dixon anxious, annoyed, and a little bit angry. He was used to traffic in the US, where people mostly only use the horn when they're upset with another driver.

Luckily, the local driver who took Dixon to his job site every day was a talkative man. Dixon took advantage of this time in the car and asked the driver questions left and right. About things he saw. Things he had experienced in Cambodia.

One day he asked the driver, "Why do people honk their horns so much when they are driving and flash their lights?"

The driver's patient answer made sense to Dixon.

"They actually have a purpose for their horn over here,"

he says. "They use their horn to let people know that they are passing. Just to let them know that they are there." Knowing the reason, Dixon felt a little less on edge.

Reflecting on your own culture can be a starting point for figuring out what you have in common with people and where you're truly different. It can give you some ideas about why people in other cultures seem strange to you. And why you seem strange to them.

Let's face it. Americans have a lot of ways and habits that strike others as just plain weird. Like an obsessive need for speed.

"The typical American mission focus and impatience of getting everything done in the first pass—I'm guilty of that myself. It's just not going to work sometimes, and it's something to be aware of," reflects Army Colonel Canon Waters.

As a China Foreign Area Officer, Waters has spent almost ten years of his life working diplomatic missions in the Far East. "Pace is important. Unfortunately, it's something we don't have. We just have one speed—fast, get it done. We're not a culture with patience. Sometimes that one speed won't get it done, and we have to be aware of that."

Yank people aboard and move out fast. Get it done yesterday. Marine Corps Colonel David Bunn understands the urgency inherent in US military culture. At the same time, his own background helps him appreciate where it's not always effective.

"My wife is from New Hampshire, and she's the friendliest woman in the world. But she'll walk in and just start talking to somebody. And I'm like, what about hello first? Or just good morning?" Bunn grew up in eastern Tennessee. To him, communicating with people in developing countries is not very different from communicating with people in the South in the US.

"I always have to explain this to people, especially Yankees. They go, 'Why can't they just say what they want to say? Why does it take so damn long?' Well. It takes an hour to say hello. And if you're not ready to make that kind of a time commitment, you're not going to accomplish anything."

Any customary way of doing things has some advantages and disadvantages. Taking a close look at yourself can help you understand your differences with others more objectively. Doing so can help you spot areas where you might be more effective by adapting some of your ways, rather than seeking to change other people.

Your thoughts about another culture, its values and its ways, impact the way you engage with people. It goes the other way too. What people think of you influences your ability to get things done. Reflecting on the cultural and historical background you come from can give you clues as to how others see you.

Other peoples' opinions don't just come from your personal history with them. They can be formed by interacting with the guys who had your job before you, or even from historical events that took place long before you were born. Understanding what happened before you got on the scene can help you figure out what your starting point is with people. And this is essential to finding a way forward.

Navy SEAL Commander Russell had been sent into Pakistan to meet with one of the country's general officers. The goal was to quickly broker an agreement to allow his unit to increase their footprint close to the Afghan border. The Pakistani government was very hesitant to do that.

"We wanted to get in there. Obviously. That was where the Taliban and al-Qaeda was. That was where bin Laden was ultimately found," Russell says.

It was the second or third time Russell had met with the general, and the two had built a good foundation of rapport. Finally, it was time to get to the pressing issue.

"So, we kind of in a very politically correct manner, we went through it, what we would like to do is ask, is there any way you could do this?" he recalls. The reply took him aback.

"'Why should I trust you and America? You told us the same thing with Gary Powers, and when he was shot down, you sold us out. So why would I believe you now?' That's what he responded," says Russell.

The Pakistani general leaned back and stared intently at him. The question hung in the silence between them while the gears inside Russell's head cranked in a hundred different directions.

He had been caught completely off guard by the general's historical reference.

"We were having this very formal meeting," he recalls. "For me, to have somebody talk about an event that happened in 1962, well before I was born, or before he was born for that matter, was . . . interesting."

Russell had read about the Gary Powers incident as a history major in college. Powers was a U-2 pilot who was shot down over the Soviet Union and captured. The relevant issue was that the US had had a secret base in Pakistan from which he was flying. This all came out after Powers was shot down, even though the US had promised Pakistan to never reveal this secret base.

Having a vague awareness of the historical context helped Russell keep his composure in the moment and formulate a response.

"I was sort of 'Yes, um, I understand your position completely. And that is very true, that event did happen. It was long before our time. Those were different general officers, different leaders. That was a different era.'"

This didn't satisfy the general, however.

"He sort of very dismissively said, 'No. I understand that

may be the case, but that is our history and I think we are done.' And so that is where we ended the meeting," says Russell.

Intrigued by the out-of-the-blue reference, Russell and his team went off and researched the Gary Powers incident. The profound lack of trust indicated by the general's question took Russell and his team by surprise.

"And I always thought it was a really interesting cultural perspective," Russell contemplates. "Here is a country that remembers everything. Whereas we, from our perspective, Americans are like, eh, what happened last Wednesday is fairly insignificant because it is Tuesday today. What is most important? The here and the now."

"We realized at that point that we were working on their timeline, not ours," he says. Understanding how strongly past historical events had colored the general's view of America helped Russell adjust his outlook and approach. Quite a bit of time would be needed to rebuild lost trust.

Along with his team, Russell went away and recalibrated the negotiation strategy and their expectations for how long it would take. Ultimately it took another year and a half to work out a deal.

Wherever you go, people are going to have thoughts about who you are, or who you might be, just based on the fact that you're an American. Their ideas might come from their country's history with the US, watching American movies, or from firsthand experiences—say, from working with other Americans in the past.

The reality is, most places you'll go aren't exactly popular tourist destinations. Which means that if they've met an ugly American, it's likely to be one of the guys you take over from. And if they thought your predecessor was loud, arrogant, and rude, then they'll probably expect you to be too. You'll have some work to do to change their view.

Good or bad, people everywhere will have some ideas about who you are before you walk in the door. And these ideas color their expectations and trust. They shape the way they interact with you and how resistant they are to your ideas. If you ignore what they're thinking about you, then you're pretty much flying blind. You'll have no idea how the things you say and do are received.

"'We know you. You're not into Thai bar girl,'" Special Agent Sean Starnes recalls, imitating a Thai accent. "That was the first thing she said to me." Starnes is describing his first meeting with his interpreter during a several-months-long assignment in Thailand.

"She said, 'Oh, I know who you are,'" he continues. "I was like, 'Really?' And she said, 'Yeah, yeah. We talk about you.'"

Starnes was astonished and a little disturbed. But he quickly realized that this was a very good thing. To the interpreter, this meant he could be trusted. It also meant that during her off hours, she didn't mind showing him around town.

"She knew it wasn't going to be a date," he says, and then explains the lesson he walked away with from this encounter.

"It's my opinion that they are watching you pretty hard, pretty close. Not in the sense that Big Brother is watching you—surveillance-like. But they are looking at you and how you react to things on the street and how you react to other people.

"And you never know when you are going to give some sort of clue or indication about your character or your agenda that may really come to help you or harm you in mission accomplishment."

Starnes goes on to describe how he has seen colleagues sit down with host nationals in restaurants, following beautiful local women walking by with their eyes. "I see it," he says. "And the host country nationals are seeing it.

"It's my sense that you always have to watch out for how you are being perceived. Holistically. Because doing business in a place like Bangkok is not the same as doing business in Charleston. Not the same playground, not the same set of rules. If I go out with the local cops here in Berkley County, I am not really worried about being set up by a prostitute or anything like that. The poorer the country, the crazier things can happen."

Knowing what people think about you can be helpful. Especially if you discover that you need to adjust their expectations. It can also give you some ideas about things that might make a positive or negative impression on them. Army Lieutenant Colonel Matthew Smith says that he, too, has learned this lesson over the years.

"For me, the lesson is, you need to understand how they view you. And how they kind of view the world. You may be the American and have this important job, but if you are still in your thirties and the other guy might be a Ukrainian lieutenant colonel who's been serving for thirty-five years, while you may have the same rank, you are younger, he is older.

"You have to operate with the assumption that you can disagree with their view but still give them a certain amount of respect."

Culture is normal. Everyone comes steeped in a culture, history, and personal background that guide how they view events. Even you. Most people in the world don't have your background. They don't think like you. They don't think like Americans. Outside of the US, people adhere to different principles and ideals. They have different considerations when they make decisions. And they don't operate on the same timelines.

So, what do you do with that?

It's your choice. You can absorb that piece of information

and think, "Well, my way is clearly the right way and they just need to change."

Or, you can instead choose to think about yourself from the outside. Use your own culture to gain a foothold in situations that throw you off your game. In doing so, you may discover that the differences aren't as insurmountable as they seem at first. And that is critical to your ability to develop the relationships you need to move forward.

Think about it this way. Say you believe the foreigners you interact with are indecent and immoral, maybe because of the way they dress. Or, say you think they're unreasonably strict, severe, and repressive. Again, maybe because of the way they dress.

This view makes you more likely to make other negative assumptions about them, which will in turn make you prone to behave more coolly, reservedly, and standoffishly around them. Creating your own barriers won't help you get things done quickly. To be efficient, you may well need to work through theirs.

Take a peek at what you look like from where they're sitting. Try to gain some insight into how they see you. What they think about you. What they feel about you. Where you are in developing rapport with them. Do they see you as big headed, boisterous, and brash because you're an American? Do they think you have infinite abilities because America is, after all, a superpower?

Once you have a sense of their views of you, you can counter the stereotypes they have about Americans and deal with their bad past experiences. You can influence those things. And turn them around if need be. You can do a clean sweep of the elephants in the room and pave the way for smoother collaboration.

Key Points

- Consider how your personal background and culture shape the way you see the world

- Objectively compare your own culture to new ones you come across

- Figure out how you and other Americans are viewed by people from other cultures

3

WORKING WITH FOREIGNERS THROUGH THE GOOD, BAD, AND BEYOND UGLY

One of Marine Corps Colonel Leonard DeFrancisci's first ventures off-base in Somalia was a trip to meet leaders of a local village. He was a major then, serving as company commander.

It was a village that had never engaged with the US military before. Getting a good relationship underway would grease the skids for the work DeFrancisci's team was going to be doing in the area.

DeFrancisci could tell that the local leadership thought the meeting was a big deal as well. They greeted the visiting Marines wearing what looked like their very best clothes.

One of the village elders offered DeFrancisci a tour of the little town. Before they set out the elder grabbed a Coke out of a cooler and handed it to DeFrancisci. He immediately noticed that the Coke was cold. The cooler had ice in it. In the middle of an African desert. DeFrancisci was impressed.

The two of them started walking through the village. After a little while they arrived at a medical clinic that had recently been stood up by a non-government group. Beaming with pride, the elder showed DeFrancisci around the tents that made up the clinic.

Suddenly the elder saw that DeFrancisci's Coke was still unopened. He snatched the bottle and reached into a bin full of used medical equipment.

"There was a pair of scissors in there, and he takes them, shakes them off, opens my Coke with them, and hands it to me. I'm thinking to myself, 'Did I just see that right? Did he just open the bottle with scissors that were used to cut dressings off all these people?'"

DeFrancisci watched the disturbing scene unfold in what seemed like warp speed. His eyes flitted back and forth between the bloody gauze and the Coke.

"My first thought is, 'I don't know if I should drink this thing, I'm probably going to die,'" he recalls.

But DeFrancisci understood that the offering was special. He knew the Coke itself was a big deal, and he had no idea where the elder might have gotten ice for the cooler in the middle of the desert.

"To him, this was probably the equivalent of a Dom Perignon," DeFrancisci muses.

Taking all this into consideration, he knew that refusing the Coke could do irreparable damage to the relationship going forward. So, DeFrancisci drank the Coke, all the while imagining himself suffering an excruciating death later. Fortunately, none of that came to be. The visit turned out to be a great success and he felt no ill effects.

DeFrancisci's ability to keep his reactions in check was seriously challenged. He was successful because he was able to set his emotions aside and draw a line between what he felt and what he was there to do.

DeFrancisci weighed the risks and possible rewards of going against his own preferences. Those calculations allowed him to momentarily insulate his actions from his feelings.

Chief Warrant Officer Duward Massey, who has found himself in similar situations more than a few times, explains what this entails: "You have to compartmentalize how you feel, and what you think, and how you see things. Put that in the back pocket and only think in terms of affecting an outcome. What is your priority? You have to let all the emotional baggage go, and really just focus on the objective."

Lieutenant Colonel Greg Heines found himself having to this more than once a day during an assignment in Russia for the Defense Threat Reduction Agency.

"It was the trip from hell," he says matter-of-factly.

"I was in charge of these unclassified reconnaissance missions over Russia. This particular time it was a joint mission with Turkey. And there was no love lost between these two countries." This relationship set the scene for a number of events that tested Heines's patience over the next several days.

"We were going to go over the Black Sea and take pictures. And, when you're doing that, there's a resolution that you aren't supposed to exceed. That means you have to fly at a certain altitude. So, on mission planning day we agreed to a flight plan—altitudes and all that. And it took about eight hours, which is a long time," he sighs.

During the flight, Heines noticed that one of the Russian flight crew members was arguing with the Turkish team leader. The volume rose rapidly, and body fluids started flying.

"These guys were yelling at each other, spitting. One was speaking Russian and the other Turkish. And of course, they didn't know what they were saying to each other, they were just yelling at each other."

Heines asked two of his sergeants, who spoke Turkish and Russian, to listen in. One quickly reported back that Heines needed to step in.

"These guys are going to go to fists, he told me. I was like, what? I got up and said, 'What is going on?'

"It turned out the Russian was saying we need to be at six thousand meters. We were at five thousand meters above the ground.

"Through the interpreter, I asked, 'Well, what did you sign on the flight plan?'"

The answer was five thousand meters.

"The Russian team chief looked like a deer in the headlights. The air traffic controllers on the ground thought that the plan was supposed to be at six thousand. There was obviously a disconnect."

The Turkish pilot made an executive decision. "He was like, no, we aren't going to six thousand, we are staying at five thousand."

But the spat continued on after.

"I remember in the lobby of this hotel, just a huge, heated discussion. I mean, basically a lot of yelling at each other. And here, the Americans, we were trying to calm them down."

When the exchange finally fizzled, everyone was exhausted from the long, conflict-filled day. The Turks turned to Heines and his team and invited them out for drinks. This would have been a nice offer, except for a tiny issue.

"The Russians had told us, 'You will not go outside, you will stay in the hotel. There is a lot of crime in this city.'

"So, we were like, nah, you guys go right ahead." The Turks went out partying that night and got back around four in the morning.

"So, they were having a good ole time, and the next

morning, of course the Russian commander calls me and the Turkish team and was like, 'I told you not to go out and you disobeyed me. You are here under a treaty. The country is responsible for your health, and it is responsible for your safety.'

"The Turk just looked at him and said, 'Eh, we will be sure not to do it next time.'"

Heines had been walking a tightrope, making sure not to take sides in the ongoing clashes between the two countries. But he did agree with the Turks on one front. The living conditions in the Russian facilities were substandard.

Working abroad for years, he was used to being served food that looked, smelled, and tasted different from what he was used to. At this installation though, he could only recognize the bread. The rest seemed unidentifiable.

"I couldn't eat my food because you don't know what you are eating. Is this rice?" he recalls. Yet, it was more than the food that sent Heines close to the edge.

"There was this light in the ceiling. It was a very plain, concrete, cold, grey Russian-looking building. There was no AC, no heat. And the light, there was this big hole where the chain and the wires went.

"There must have been a hundred bees going in and out of that hole. So, we were eating breakfast and the bees were flying over our breakfast. Well, a bee climbs up my flight suit and I get stung," he says with amazement.

That was the final straw. "I walked out. I am not eating it. I am not eating here, there are bees all over. It was insane."

The Turks had been particularly animated about voicing their displeasure. And, as the end of the assignment neared, the Turks got wind that the Russians were planning to complain about the Turks' late-night drinking in their final comments on the mission plan.

"This is an agreement all countries have to sign, documenting that the mission was successful," Heines explains.

Upset about the Russians' negative comments, the Turkish mission commander asked Heines if he would put some comments in about the food not being acceptable.

"I said 'No, I am not putting in those comments.' Why not? I wanted to keep it non-political.

"We know that the standard of living in Russia is lower than in the United States. So, I am not going to rub it in their face that yeah, when we were eating breakfast bees were coming out of the walls and stinging us. Nah, I am not going to do that.

"My job was to get pictures and get them home. If I got stung by a couple of bees in the process, oh, well."

Keeping your goals and your mission at the forefront of your mind, as Heines did, can help you manage your reactions and attitudes. Ask yourself this: Are your personal feelings more important than your mission? Your personal feelings can get in the way of developing relationships with people. And these relationships can get you closer to meeting your objectives.

That isn't always enough, though. Sometimes, other people's values and preferences hit you in a way that truly and deeply tests your resolve. Sometimes, the things foreigners do and say aren't just rude or offensive. They feel wrong in the worst way. In those cases, the thought of continuing to smile, nod, and build rapport will make your stomach churn.

For Army Captain Blair, some of the things his foreign partners did took the meaning of disgust to a whole new level.

Blair had been working, training, and conducting missions with an Afghan Army unit. He had nothing against goat meat. In fact, he found it rather tasty. So much so that after the unit had performed especially well on a mission, he rewarded them by buying them three goats. He expected that the men would be able to cook several nice meals in the coming weeks.

The following day he noticed that all three goats had been slaughtered. Puzzled, he approached Patman, the leader of the unit, to find out why. He was told that Patman had personally slaughtered the animals.

"Wouldn't it have been better to slaughter and eat them one by one to keep the meat fresh?" Blair asked.

Patman lowered his eyes. Blair knew the man as

devoutly religious and a tough but fair leader.

Patman reluctantly revealed that some of his men had been having too much fun with the goats. A little party. He wanted it to end. So, he slaughtered them all.

"He then proceeded to offer me a plate with the goat meat." Blair says with an uneasy laugh.

As Blair finishes describing this baffling exchange, it becomes clear that he can't decide which was more disturbing: the men's activities with the goats, or the thought of eating the meat from one of them afterwards.

Situations like this, which leave you speechless, can paralyze your willingness to engage with people. How can you look them in the eye, let alone shake their hand? Failing to find a way to move past the ugliness, though, can become an obstacle to accomplishing your mission.

How did Blair do it?

He shifted his attention away from the goats and on to Patman. Blair had come to develop a genuine respect for the man over the past months. The way he handled the goat situation was in line with his general tendency to take swift and decisive action.

This was a trait Blair appreciated, and that made him feel Patman was someone he could rely on, should they find themselves in a tough situation down range. Reframing the situation this way helped Blair repair his will and motivation for keeping his working relationship with the Afghan unit going.

At times, setting your own feelings aside can feel impossible. In those situations, thinking about ways to reframe the situation can be an effective strategy. You create an alternative way to look at the situation or relationship. Finding a silver lining or a positive side to an otherwise disturbing situation is an effective way to minimize the negative impact.

One way to reframe when working overseas is to consider the cultural aspect of the behaviors you experience. When you're working with foreigners, many of the things they do that you find rude and unpleasant have nothing to do with you. That is, they aren't doing them because it's their objective to be rude or mean to you; they're not aware that their behavior is going to have a negative effect on you. It helps to keep that in mind.

Recognizing when what you're seeing or hearing is part of their culture can sometimes help you not take people's behavior personally. This worked well for Army Master Sergeant Carson in Afghanistan. Carson quickly found himself frustrated working with Afghans.

"They said they would do something and nine times out of ten they wouldn't follow through. They just didn't keep their word," he laments.

He remained aggravated until he came across some information about the Pashtunwali code. Reading it, Carson realized that to the Pashtuns he was dealing with, to refuse help, even when they didn't think they could help, would be considered rude and inhospitable.

"It kind of gave me a gauge for some of their actions," he says. "I found that when I couched it within Pashtunwali and how they abided by that, I didn't find it as offensive, like, to me personally. I found that that's their code, that's what they abide by, and that's how they do that. And so, it was easier for me to accept it in that particular context."

If you discover that the reasons for a behavior relate to culture, you might find that it's not as dishonest, distasteful, or disagreeable as you first thought, because now you know it's not something they're doing to aggravate or annoy you personally.

Even though it can seem difficult at times, try to maintain a positive, or at least neutral, attitude toward the culture. Building and maintaining rapport is easier if you can balance the number of things that rub you the wrong way with things that you like or respect about the people you interact with.

Look for a positive. Something you could put in the pro column if you were making a pros and cons list about the people or the culture. That goes for cultural groups as well as individuals.

For example, Army Lieutenant Colonel Mike Holmes has had three tours in Afghanistan and has also spent time in Iraq and Kosovo. If you ask him about Afghans, he says,

"(They are) incredibly ingenious. There was not a single thing that these Afghans could not build. They can make anything with a hunk of metal and a file. I respected the hell out of them, I really did. I liked them a lot."

It's completely normal to like some aspects of a foreign culture and absolutely detest others. The danger is that it can be easy to fall into the trap of spending a lot of your time thinking about the negatives. They can seem to slap you in the face sometimes. To counteract the tendency of things you don't like dominating your headspace, try focusing on some positives.

Sounds simple, right? But it's not always easy. Not remotely. In those cases, it can sometimes help to take a step back.

Master Gunnery Sergeant Rodgers has been a Marine for twenty-five years. A quarter century of his life has been spent in various corners of the world. Some dark, some less so. Rodgers reflects at length about how amazing many of his experiences abroad have been.

"Israel was just beautiful," he says wistfully. He found the atmosphere and architecture in Italy to be phenomenal. The Moroccans to be extremely kind and courteous people. The Turks were gracious. He found Koreans to be admirably resilient and determined. Plus, their food was so delicious he had to watch his weight. In Iraq, he enjoyed that many of his counterparts were well educated, and thorough in their thought patterns and decision making.

It's clear Rodgers has made an effort look for positive experiences everywhere he's been. But parts of Southeast Asia knocked him sideways.

"It was a disgusting place to me, ethically speaking," he says. A particular experience in Thailand stands out.

A Marine sergeant in Rodgers's unit had been guarding a pallet of water bottles. Good, fresh, clean water, which was at a premium. A man rode up to him on a bicycle; two little girls walked beside him.

The sergeant guessed that the man must be the father of the girls, who looked to be eleven or twelve years old. "The father offered one of his daughters to my sergeant for two cases of water," Rodgers says. It's obvious that the thought still bothers him.

Rodgers has thought about this encounter many times. He hasn't found a way to cast the activities he saw in Southeast Asia in a positive light. But instead he has taken a step back and placed them within a broader context.

As he puts it, "You have to look at the entirety of the environment that you are in. Some of the cultures that you interact with are very fragile. People are kind of like a wounded dog in some regards. They will want to lash out, but they really don't mean it. They are just hurting."

Thinking of it this way has helped him soften his frustration with certain things people did, as well the ways they sometimes reacted toward him.

If you can't find a silver lining, take a step back. Zoom out and look at the big picture. It might give you a way to reframe or repackage what you're seeing so that it doesn't fuel your anger or jab you in the heart as much as it otherwise would.

When you're in the heat of the moment, you might not always have the time or energy to truly process what's happening. The best you can do is simply set the bad stuff aside. After a while, though, it can start feeling like you've been hitting the "Off" button on your moral compass too many times—like you're not being true to yourself and the things you believe in.

Pull those rough experiences you've shelved out again later. Dust them off and try to find a different way to look at them. See if you can find a silver lining or make a cultural connection. And if you can't, at least try to look at the big picture. Try to put things in context.

It can also help to keep in mind that the way you feel is not necessarily about what the people around you are doing. It's shaped by things that are going on with you.

Your feelings towards a culture, or aspects of it, will change naturally over time. This can work in a positive way. Things that feel horrible and offensive at first may suddenly not seem that awful anymore. Maybe it's because you get used to seeing them. Or maybe you start understanding them better.

It can go the other way too. Sometimes, the wear and strain of adapting yourself to another culture takes its toll. Army Sergeant First Class Armenio has seen this a lot.

"At the end of tours, you become physically and psychologically fatigued, your frustration tolerance seems to diminish, and you're exhausted. When that happens, sometimes it becomes easy to criticize, and you tend to be somewhat harsher than you might generally be. And you know it's the frustration of trying very diligently, working hard, long hours and not necessarily seeing anything tangible resulting from it."

When this happens, taking a timeout can help you continue to work with people.

As Marine Lieutenant Ober puts it, maybe you need to "go smoke a cigarette somewhere else. I mean, I've been there. It can be frustrating. But . . . maybe you need to go take a break.

"If you're on their dirt you got to do things their way even if it's not the way you want to. Because if you start getting in the way and changing how you deal with them, all it's going to do is make you and your successor look bad."

Losing your grip and letting things get to you can make things go south in a hurry.

"I didn't even have to sit down, I saw he was flying off the handle right away and I was like, OK, shit, there is no way around this." Army Colonel Beck realized this immediately when he walked into a meeting room at Ft. Benning.

A delegation of Iraqi government officials and military leadership were meeting with foreign military sales reps to discuss a purchase of combat vehicles. A US lieutenant colonel was facilitating the engagement.

Beck had popped in the room to say hello, knowing that he'd worked with some of the Iraqis on his previous tours.

"In the middle of their questioning, my lieutenant colonel just flatly interrupted them and said, 'No, you are not going to ask those questions because we've already answered them.'

"That was my signal that I had to stop him," Beck recalls. The Iraqis were less than amused, and they were not buying it. Beck was going to have to stay to turn things around.

Beck knew that the lieutenant colonel had been working with the Iraqis for eleven months prior to this meeting.

"He was just very frustrated, and it's just an interesting dynamic I noticed. I witnessed it on every American and every Brit that we had over there at that time working with the Iraqis. Your personality and the way you deal with them would change at about the ninth to tenth month mark, because you just had enough."

The lieutenant colonel had lost his patience.

"He treated them like Americans. He never let them be Iraqi. You had a discussion once. You got your answer, move out. And sometimes you do have to be that way. But it wasn't working in this case, and he was kind of overcome by it."

It's inevitable. To be successful working with foreigners, you'll need to adjust and do things differently than the ways you're used to. It may not seem like that big of a deal at first. But the effects of making this kind of adjustment can sneak up on you slowly. Eventually, it can start to gnaw at you.

You can temper the effects by recognizing how situations affect your reactions, and by finding ways to break away and recharge. Calibrating your expectations to match realities on the ground can also go a long way towards alleviating your frustration.

"The locals were on what they call African Standard Time." Sergeant Armenio smiles as he talks about his experiences in Djibouti.

"They just have a pliable matrix and temporal demands are really not something they adhere to on a regular basis. People who open up shops don't open them up at the same time every day. They'll open them when they get there. And when they get there is largely determined by a number of other things, not all under their control. The pace of life is different."

When working abroad, you may well need to adjust

your notions of how much you can accomplish. Army Sergeant Jones thinks about it this way: You have to temper your expectations, otherwise you'll be disappointed.

"Kenyans, for example, they are probably some of the best-equipped dudes in the African union," he says. "But they still are going to have some logistics issues.

"I need to make sure that I know that when I ask for something, it's not coming for three weeks. In doing that, I'm tempering my own expectations and I'm not going to be doing the classic American thing where I wanted it yesterday. Cause that's not going to get done. I need to make sure I'm working on their time and their capabilities."

When you have disturbing and downright dreadful experiences abroad, it's easy to get thrown off your game. You get frustrated and upset in the moment, and over time you might even become permanently mad at the world.

So what? How you feel is your prerogative, right?

The problem is that it's nearly impossible to keep your aggravation hidden. This can be a major stumbling block to building rapport and relationships with people and therefore to getting things done.

You can fall into the same rut even if you haven't experienced anything personally horrifying or horrendous. Instead maybe you've heard stories that make you feel uneasy. Or you've learned some things about the culture that rub you the wrong way.

Be picky about the voices and perspectives you take to heart. When someone's giving you their view on things, consider how it affects your overall perceptions. If it's a bleak, cynical, or depressing view, it will likely prevent you from getting in a frame of mind where you can build relationships and meet your objectives.

Instead, try to find ways to reframe events, or cast people and cultures in a positive or constructive light. Whatever positive points you discover, find out more about them, or spend some time thinking more about them.

Maybe you discover that the locals are extremely hospitable. What does hospitality mean for them? How do they show it?

Dwelling on the positive a little longer will help you counterweigh the negative.

Key Points

- Manage your reactions and attitudes to sustain relationships and get things done

- Find ways to maintain a positive or neutral attitude toward the culture

- Notice how broader, ongoing circumstances are affecting your attitudes and reactions

4

A FUN WAY TO LEARN
ABOUT NEW CULTURES

What's the best way to get up to speed on a new culture?

Come to class. Take some notes. Done.

You're ready!

Unfortunately, it's not that simple. You can't expect to learn everything you'll need to know about culture in a classroom. There's just too much information to cover.

Plus, the initial overview you get will likely be fairly generic. It's a great starting point. But you need information that's a little more personalized. To do that, you have to put some skin in the game.

"My take is that my cultural training never stops," says Marine Corps Colonel Hanson. "My assumption is that people who try to train me before I go do the best they can. But it's undoubtedly incomplete and in some cases inaccurate. So, I try to immerse myself as much as I can into the culture and begin to flesh it out by what I see and by the people I interact with."

Staff Sergeant Aaronson, an Army aircraft structural repairer who's spent almost a decade of his life overseas, couldn't agree more. "A course can give me a good baseline, and I take it for what it's worth. I wouldn't frame all my interactions with the locals based on just everything I've been taught in a course, because a course is never going to teach you the little nuances of a culture."

In Aaronson's experience, most of the information he needs to engage effectively across cultures he finds for himself. "If you want to endear yourself to the locals, instead of saying this basic phrase that you learned out of this book, find out what they actually say. That's stuff you have to pick up on your own."

Any one course or class can't possibly cover everything there is to know about a foreign culture. It can't prepare you for every strange, ambiguous, potentially awkward situation you're likely to find yourself in.

Learning about culture isn't a one-time deal. It's not just attending a briefing or reading as much as you can on the web, and then you're done. It's an ongoing self-guided voyage, and you're the captain. It starts before you travel anywhere, really picks up speed during your stay, and continues even after you return.

That may sound daunting. How do you even start, when there's just so much information? And what should you be trying to learn?

Cross-cultural SMEs have an advantage. They know how they'll be using the things they learn about a new culture. They know what information preserves their life and sanity, so they look for that information first. An excellent starting point is to focus on knowledge that will help you build rapport and develop relationships.

Finding cultural information that helps with relationships can be easy, fun even. To start, follow your own interests. Give yourself the freedom to explore on your own and make the journey enjoyable. Think about what you like to do and talk about at home and see how it maps on to your destination. You'll feel more motivated to learn and be more sincere in conversation.

"When you're talking to people, you have to do the best you can to show a genuine interest in the topic, you know, whatever it is," says Navy Master Chief Petty Officer Dale Carter. "You have to be able to personalize it."

Next, branch out to get a little background to help you understand what makes locals in your new area tick, how they think. Then, dig deeper to get the inside scoop on life in the region. Try to understand where the locals are coming from. Finally, learn a few cultural nuggets to show your interest in the people you're living among. Each of these will help you form closer ties and partnerships, while keeping your learning load light.

Picture this: You've just arrived in Angola. Your local

counterparts are putting on a lavish welcome banquet. You're the guest of honor. Weirdly, only you and the senior Angolan Army officer, a general, seem to be eating anything.

You're standing next to the general. The other Angolan soldiers huddle along the walls, talking amongst themselves. No one approaches. The general says nothing. He chews. Silence. More chewing. Ouch.

Navy Lieutenant Commander Owens faced the silent general in Angola.

"I would have expected in that situation, maybe somebody come up to talk to me or something," he says. "But everybody kind of stayed back and it was just me and the general that stood there. Away from everyone else. And he didn't say anything. I had to initiate the conversation."

The Algeria assignment was Owens's first after completing his in-country training as a foreign area officer. In Brazil.

Back home, college football had decorated Owens's TV most nights. But he had gotten into watching soccer while he was in South America. Soccer is a big deal in Brazil. He'd kept up on the sport because he'd learned that it was popular in Africa as well.

"So, I started asking him about the soccer games going on, the World Cup," he recalls. Bringing it up seemed to work. "He did end up talking about that a little more," says

Owens. "It broke the pain. That was probably the only point that there was any kind of lighter mood, where we were able to talk with breaking a smile."

Take a minute to think about what gets your juices flowing. You're a sports buff? You're into card games, computer games, cars, music? Hunting? History? Think about topics you can talk about with genuine enthusiasm. Whether you're going to Angola, Afghanistan, or Azerbaijan, you're going to meet people who share your passion. Even if it's knives.

Army Staff Sergeant Knowles has a keen interest in knives. Before heading to Afghanistan, he did some research on Afghan knives and knife-making practices. Chooras, Khyber salawars, and lohars, to pick a few. And while in country, he took every opportunity to discuss knifemaking with local Afghans.

Do a little research on local flavors of your fancy. Get the lowdown on what an Angolan fill-in-the-blank fan is into. If it's sports, are they into football? No.

Futsal. What is that?

You discover that the Futsal World Cup is next week. Focusing on things that interest you will help you tune into easy opportunities to chat. Maybe you overhear your interpreters talk about the World Cup. Or maybe your counterpart has a sticker from the local futsal team on his bag.

When you strike up a conversation about your favorite topic, you'll sound more intelligent and more interesting. That's a ready-made connection. The groundwork is laid for solid trust right there. It will also make doing a bit of research on your own much more pleasant.

In addition to mapping your interests to the local culture, aim to get a better sense of how people think. The stories people tell each other and their children can help you gain an inside perspective.

Navy SEAL Commander Russell pinpointed a sliver of time in the day where he could squeeze in a few minutes of culture reading. For himself *and* his men.

"I put copies of Ethiopian fables in the bathrooms," he says.

Russell's men had little free time when they were on assignment in Ethiopia. Also, they weren't all that interested in culture. But he knew that it was important for them to understand what the people in the area were like. What made them tick. The stories were so compelling that he didn't even have to encourage discussion.

"They were awesome. The guys loved them. I told them, 'You can read one in the morning, one in the evening and you're done.' And they did.

"And then they would talk about them because they were fun. It was like, 'Oh my god did you read the one about the little girl?'

"and they'd be like, 'Yeah, that was great!' or 'No, I haven't read that one. Don't, don't, don't talk about it yet.'"

Russell realized that there's a time and place for handbooks, instruction manuals, and academic texts. And that luckily, there are other ways to learn about culture. Ways that may even get you up close and personal with a new culture faster than textbooks can.

"It doesn't have to be a seven-hundred-page, six-volume thesis on the history of the Ethiopian tribes," Russell says. "It could be a movie on that topic, if there is such a movie. It could be a collection of short stories or even commercials. You know, what's on their TV that shows their families and how they interact. It's amazing to watch that."

Look for information that gives you more direct access to what's on people's minds. That's the quickest way to figure out where they are coming from. Good stories, like fables, can do that. But they can also be found in fiction books, TV shows, podcasts, even jokes. Google *Angolan humor*, or look for Angolan standup on YouTube.

Humor, especially satire, reveals what people care about. A quick Google-tour of Angolan comic strips shows that Angolans joke about the influence the Chinese have on the country, lack of high-speed internet, and the slowness of public services.

Reading fiction is fun, and it can be helpful. Army Major Lino Miani explains: "Because when you're reading a story about human interaction and things like that, it illustrates relationships better than a pocket guide on the culture. And because it's a story, it sort of sticks with you."

Books, TV programs, movies. Whether you're into fables, comedy, poetry, drama, mystery, horror, fantasy, science fiction, detective stories, or graphic novels, you're bound to find something you find interesting. (And yes, there really is such a thing as an Ethiopian science-fiction movie.)

You can learn from fiction, even if it's a genre you usually think of as leaving you dumber than you were going in. The trick is to look for resources that are created by and for locals—fiction that's produced by authors from the region, for people in the region.

"One strategy I think really helped me in Syria," says Kinney, a National Security Education Program scholar. "I watched this soap opera that everyone watched. It's a great way to learn what people are going through, but in a more emotional kind of experiential way, through the characters themselves."

"In a way, that's culture right there, being produced," Kinney adds. You'll see what makes them angry, what makes them sad, and what makes them laugh.

You explored topics that interest you personally, and you dove into some popular culture to learn more about what makes locals tick. Next, getting the inside scoop on everyday life in the area is also useful for fostering relationships. Knowing more about where people are coming from makes it easier to interact and work with them.

Even before you head out, people who can give you an inside scoop on the culture you'll be operating in are all around. Talk to them. Try to figure out what the world looks like from where they're sitting. You're only limited by your imagination, and your willingness to start a conversation.

Whether you're in Alabama, North Carolina, or Arizona, there are people around you from all over the world. Foreign partners, exchange students, drivers, cooks, janitors, secretaries. You can get lucky and find someone on post, or you might have to venture off.

Marine Sergeant Ben Kennedy has made it a habit to visit an ethnic restaurant or two before he ships out.

"Let's say we're going to Algeria, for example. I'll go out to an Algerian restaurant. Talk to the waiter or the guy behind the bar. I think that's the best way to find out about a culture. You need somebody who can talk about what they talk about, what they think about, what their ideals are. They can also tell you things like, 'Hey, if you see a bar with a red *X* on top, that's a sign to stay the fuck out.'

"In my mind, the waiter's experiences and opinions are much more valuable than someone who is getting paid to tell me about the culture. And it's more interesting, because that person has no agenda and nothing to lose." Kennedy seeks out people with first-hand knowledge of a foreign culture or region because they can give him information he's unlikely to find on a webpage or in a book.

Maybe you like the idea of getting some insight by talking to people who've lived in the culture, but you're not able to find the right folks in your area. Then check them out on the web. You can tap into people's thoughts any place they share their point of view.

The internet is full of people with a lot of time on their hands yakking away about anything and everything, and they're from anywhere you can imagine. Danes, Poles, Egyptians, Iraqis, Colombians, Somalis. You name it. People putting it all out there. Telling you their innermost thoughts. You can remain a casual observer. Or you can get involved. Ask them some questions.

Army Sergeant First Class Ahmed heard that people in Ghana shake hands in a weird way. Curious, he turned to an online discussion forum.

"When they shake hands, they snap their fingers. And I didn't know why they did that. So, I asked in a blog, why do you guys do that, why do you snap your fingers once you detach your hand from the other person's hands?

"Someone told me that it was during the slavery time, that they used to cut the slaves' fingers. And they started doing that to show that hey, I am not a slave."

There's a lot you can learn before you hit the ground on a foreign assignment, and once you get on the ground, your learning can really pick up speed. People who know more than you do about the local culture, region, and language will be all around—interpreters, counterparts, taxi drivers, neighbors, and rug salesmen.

In Albania, Marine Corps Colonel Louis Boros found several people around him to hit up for some insight into the culture.

"Just simply talking to the locals. It's amazing what they will tell you. I live in an apartment here in Albania, and my landlord is a young entrepreneur. He runs an IT company. I have people around me all day long, many of whom speak very good English. I talk to them. I talk to them about what their concerns are, why they do what they do, what they think, how they think, and so on."

General Anthony Zinni is a many-time decorated war hero. He speaks Vietnamese, Italian, and a little bit of French and Arabic. He can't even count how many languages he can order food in.

Since retiring, he's been called upon by the US government and the international community to mediate high-stakes, high-profile conflict negotiations countless times. He's widely recognized as an expert on using cultural understanding to accomplish national-security objectives. He's a big believer in talking to people in all walks of life to understand the problem spaces you're working in.

"I own a hundred and twenty-three oriental rugs," Zinni says with a big smile, "because I would go to my oriental-rug dealers and I would drink tea, smoke the hookah, you know. Sit around and talk to them and say, 'Ali, tell me about life on the street? Tell me what people are thinking.'

"When I was a commander at CENTCOM, I met the elites. I heard from the elites, the leadership," Zinni explains. "I want a sense of the people on the street. You need a little sense of that because what you're doing is going to be affected by that view. It's not just what the politicians are telling you.

"When I was doing the Israeli-Palestinian peace negotiations, I would eat dinner in East Jerusalem one night and in West Jerusalem the other."

Making a habit of finding out more about the people and cultures you're living among helps you understand what their daily life is like. It gives you a sense of what's going through their heads when you're working with them.

Picking up a few cultural nuggets is also an excellent way to show interest. Demonstrating that you know a little bit about the local culture and language shows that you cared enough to learn, which further helps you build rapport. It doesn't have to be complicated.

Navy Lieutenant Commander Kelly has found that when he goes overseas, he often runs into people who have the impression that Americans aren't all that interested in other cultures. He makes it a point to learn a few words in the local language to break that perception.

"It's like *please* and *thank you*. It's kind of the basics like that. Being able to be polite. You know, kind of be professional about how you're doing things instead of just pointing. It does go a little way to show them that you've learned a couple of words of their language.

"They're like 'OK, you're not just the stereotypical ugly American. You kind of went at least a little bit out of your way,'" Kelly explains.

Stepping into a new culture with a few questions is another way to show interest. As you do a bit of reading on the culture and region you're going into, keep an eye out for things that seem puzzling or personally interesting to you. Turn them into questions.

The first time Army Captain Ryan Casper went to Afghanistan, he wondered, "Why is the Blue Mosque in Mazar-i-Sharif blue?" He made it a point to ask a local. Don't be shy. Ask away and show them you care.

"Too many people get worried about coming across ignorant. Man, I will ask as many questions as I need to until I understand something," says Army Captain Kovach.

Questions can be great conversation starters. Plus, letting people teach you things gives them a little authority, which creates goodwill. Marine Corps Major Paul

Sotomayor has honed this strategy across his many assignments in South America.

"I ask them, tell me about this aspect of the local area. That puts them in the position of power, so to speak, because they know more than I do. I just sit back and gather that information and help build them up to that point where they feel free to talk about anything."

Asking some questions and using local greetings can be a great tactic. It shows your curiosity and that you're willing to make an effort to smooth over differences. Once you're comfortable, you can take it a little bit further.

How about learning a few phrases that help you make a deeper connection—that show your depth, your character? Phrases that show off your genuine personality and your humor. The trick is to learn expressions the locals won't expect you to know—a native idiom, proverb, or a quirky expression. "This is crap." "It doesn't matter to me." "Is this normal?" "What's up?"

When he was in Iraq, Marine Corps Major Carillo made sure he learned some key phrases he could use to break the tension in situations where people might be stressed or on edge. He and his colleagues had been given pointy-talky cards.

"They're language survival kits, where it's like a little three by five index-card-type packet. You flip through it and you'll find a bunch of phrases with the English and you'll see the Iraqi transliteration into phonetic form," he explains. Carillo found the cards helpful, but he wanted some phrases that could help him lighten the mood.

"I supplemented the pointy-talky cards with about a sheet of paper or two . . . with a bunch of Iraqi phrases that were more like social lubrication than anything else. Sayings like, 'See you again tomorrow,' or there was one which, essentially translated to, 'This is frustrating and useless,' which turned out to be *yapsi tibin*,' it's 'rice over beans,' or 'beans over rice,' just let it get done."

To get your local phrases right, find a cultural guide when you get on the ground. It can be an interpreter, a waiter at a restaurant, or the line server in the mess hall. Tell them what you want to do and let them give you some pointers. Pull these phrases out for real when you need to get someone's attention.

Maybe you learned how to say, "The squirrel does not talk back to the elephant" in Portuguese. Hearing a foreigner deliver a gem like that is massively amusing. Making people laugh can lighten the mood and tighten connections.

Learning never ends, and your cultural learning shouldn't either. Take it as far as you want. On Major Brewer's second tour in Afghanistan, the Marine Corps was conducting operations in battle space that was technically controlled by the Italians. "I was sent out to sit on the staff of the Italians, so that I could be the face of the Americans for them," he explains.

Brewer loves languages and saw this as an opportunity to deepen his Italian. He drew his Italian counterparts in as impromptu teachers, and as a result built stronger bonds with them.

"I literally set up a chalkboard, just, like, one of those butcher-block-big pieces of paper. I said, ok, this is my 'Italian word of the day board,' and every day I would ask my friends across the hall to give me a new Italian expression or an Italian verb or something. They were all tickled pink that I was taking it seriously. One of them gave me an Italian book as a gift."

Start your personal learning journey before you head out. Keep it going after you touch down. Once you get on the ground, the possibilities become virtually endless. People who can teach you about the culture are literally everywhere.

Cultural learning is an ongoing process. Yet it doesn't have to take over everything else and crowd out other important activities. You can slip culture in between the cracks. As Marine Corps Major Watson puts it, "You can learn about culture when you're not getting shot at."

Whether it's before or during your deployment, visit an ethnic restaurant, watch a local soap opera, read a collection of fables. Start with an area that sounds cool to you. See where that takes you. Make it easy on yourself to learn and to use what you've picked up in conversations.

Look for information you can use to grease the skids and to develop tighter, closer, more-trusting working relationships with the locals and foreign partners. Set an objective to learn information you can use to build rapport.

Learning more about where people are coming from is the first step to figuring out how to build bonds, earn respect, and create win-win solutions to the problems you're there to solve.

Key Points

- Take charge of your cultural learning and tailor it to your interests

- Focus your learning on building rapport and developing relationships

- Keep learning. Continually improve your cultural knowledge

5

WILL YOUR CULTURAL KNOWLEDGE SURVIVE A REALITY CHECK?

"I spent six months in Kyrgyzstan," says Air Force Senior Master Sergeant Shaun Krautkremer. "It's right below Kazakhstan, bordering China. I don't think Russia quite touches it. But it's close."

Krautkremer was in Kyrgyzstan to support a humanitarian assistance mission, repairing and building hospitals and schools. The translators the unit had brought with them spoke mainly Russian.

"The further we went out, that became a problem," he says. "They all spoke Kurdish as a language. But some had learned Russian in school. So, when we got up there to some of the further outlying villages, we had to look around for someone who spoke Russian."

After returning from the assignment, Krautkremer found himself at the Senior NCO Academy with an assignment to put together a deployment brief to somewhere he'd worked.

"I just picked Kyrgyzstan because that was the last place I had been," he says. A memorable insight struck him as he did his research on the region.

"I got onto the CIA website and they said they speak 65 percent Kyrgyz, 19 percent Russian. Nothing about Kurdish. And I was like, huh, not where I was. I was like, where are you getting this information?

Now I have to speculate the next time I look some place up, and they say they speak whatever, 80 percent Spanish, when I go down to South America. That could turn out not to be true. I am going to have to second guess. It might be true in the country, but not necessarily in the area you are going."

You hit the books, checked some facts on the internet. You even made connections with some locals. Talked to them and dug into the culture in various ways. You learned a lot. Then it happens. An event that shakes the foundation of your newfound expertise.

You realize that some of the "facts" you found don't match up with reality. In some cases, they even run counter to what you're seeing. When this happens, it can feel like ground truth is suddenly made of sand, constantly shifting under your feet. How do you regain your bearings and get a grasp on what's real?

There is one reality you can count on. General information you find about a culture might be true in some situations, but not others. General statistics or demographics about a region may not be precise enough to capture what you'll find in a specific district, village, or valley. Similarly, cultural facts and rules about how people from a culture generally think and behave do not necessarily apply all the time. They don't hold up in all situations and circumstances.

"It's ironic. You could go anywhere in Afghanistan, and you'd see the soles of the feet," Marine Captain Wisnewski says. "It's like every norm that I was told was broken in some capacity."

Marine Corps Lieutenant Colonel Mike Carter quickly became suspicious of that same cultural rule while deployed in Iraq.

"Going through training, they'd tell us, 'If they see the bottom of your feet, that's automatically an offense.'"

Carter remembers thinking to himself, "Well, OK. That's pretty extreme."

So, when he got on the ground in Iraq, he asked his interpreter about the rule, who clarified it for him. "He goes, 'They know that you don't mean to be disrespectful. But just don't automatically show the bottom of your feet if you're sitting down cross-legged,'" Carter recalls.

Going forward Carter did try to make an effort when he sat cross-legged, and he apologized if his attempts left his soles visible. "They would say, 'No, we know, you're Americans . . . we don't take this as an offense.'" Carter found that breaking this rule wasn't a big problem in his area. At least not when he was the one breaking it.

People sometimes make exceptions to their cultural rules and customs. Whether a rule is followed can depend on the specific situation. Is it a formal or informal occasion? It can also depend on whether you're there, because the locals know that you're not a member of their culture. They know that you have different customs and expectations, and they know that you might have stiff legs and wouldn't be comfortable sitting that way.

Marine Corps Major Sage experienced this in Afghanistan. He got several culture briefings about the country and culture before he headed out. One of the topics was how to conduct meetings.

"In all the cultural classes there's a big, like, 'How's your family?' You don't get to business right away. This isn't America. In America you get right down to business, and here you have to soften them up," he recalls.

"I was surprised," Sage admits, "it was quite the opposite. I mean it couldn't be more wrong. They first treated you like a business partner and, eventually, would treat you like a friend. When they didn't know you, it was very much 'Here's what I want to talk to you about.' It came right up front. Eventually, when you gained a relationship with them, *then* they'd say, 'How are things? Do you have a wife?'"

Broad guidance for a culture won't always hold up. It doesn't always apply in the specific areas you find yourself. This can create a disconnect between what you've learned and what you see on the ground.

The distortion doesn't stop there. Any one source of information you might consult is bound to have some bias. No matter if your source is your interpreter, a professor, a book, a pamphlet, a website, or what have you. All information is ultimately filtered through human experience. That means it's colored by the way the person who produced it sees the world.

"Uzbeks are shifty. You have to watch your back in dealing with them. That's what he told me," says Army Captain Ryan Casper. Casper had asked Badih, his unit's assigned interpreter, for a rundown of the different Afghan tribes.

Badih was a hugely likeable guy, who knew more about football than many Americans Casper had come across. Plus, he was a Category 1, an Afghan national, so Casper figured he must know the local people and culture pretty well.

Casper had done his due diligence. He had done a bit of research before he deployed. Once on the ground, he had made connections with some locals. He kept asking lots of questions. He was learning a lot. Except some days it felt like he was taking one step forward and two steps back.

Things that seemed like ground truth one day turned out to be completely invalidated the next.

Take for example that tidbit Badih shared about Uzbeks. A week later Casper talked to a colleague, SFC Sanchez, who was on his third tour. Together, they dug into relationships and connected some dots. Badih was a Pashtun, and it was common for Pashtuns to have an intense dislike for Uzbeks.

Badih meant no harm. He was just telling it how it was from where he was sitting. It's something we all do, at least to some extent. We bend information we encounter to fit our own frame of reference. Often, without a second's worth of thought. It shapes our language when we talk and write and even the way we report statistics.

It helps to keep in mind that there's a bit of bias in your sources of information. Not necessarily a lot, or with any nefarious intention. So, keep your eyes peeled to make sure the cultural insights you use to make critical decisions are dependable. Hold on to a little skepticism, even when you have good reasons to believe that the source in front of you is reliable.

Maybe you have a solid informant who is likely to give you up-to-date, accurate, where-the-rubber-meets-the-road kind of information. Someone like a skilled interpreter, a university professor, or someone who's spent a lot of time working in the area you're going into. Their knowledge will still have a few gaps and a slight slant, just because they're human. That's not to say you can't vet your advisors. Some will be better than others.

Army Special Forces Major Lino Miani has traveled all over the world in his military career. Europe, the Middle East, and Asia. Thailand, Malaysia, Korea. At one juncture, he found himself in Central Africa for four and a half months as part of a Humanitarian Assistance and Disaster Response team. Chad, to be specific.

"It was late one night, and me and my buddy found ourselves in a tent talking to this Swiss guy, a middle-aged gentleman who was one of the field managers of the NGO operation there," Miani recalls.

"We were kind of in awe of him. We were thinking to ourselves 'Wow, we've been here two months and we're already exhausted. This guy's been here for eighteen months and he must know everybody and all of the culture and all of the language and all of this stuff and he must really know what he's doing here."

The guys were shooting the breeze and sharing joys and woes of a globetrotting lifestyle. The Swiss wearily admitted that he couldn't wait to go back to Switzerland. Then, he made a statement that instantly revealed to Miani that the man's understanding of the local region and culture likely wasn't as deep as he'd expected.

"He tells us, 'The first thing I'm going to do is have a beer,'" Miani recollects.

"So, we were like, why don't you just have a beer here?

"He kind of looked at us like we were completely bonkers, and he said, 'Look around you, man. Where in the hell are you going to get a beer out here?'"

That's when Miani realized that this guy likely had never actually had a real conversation with an African. It just so happened that earlier that day, Miani had engaged in some cultural learning on his own.

It hadn't been a great day. Miani had received some bad news from home and found himself in profound need of a beer. Yet beer, especially a cold variety, wasn't all that easy to come by in Chad. So, he tracked down a young African colleague he'd been working with and asked him where he might find such an elusive beverage.

The young man immediately volunteered to go get some.

"I gave him some money, and off he went. I gotta tell you, we're a two-day drive from the nearest airfield. I mean, just to set the scene for you, no running water, electricity only by generator. There's no such thing as a convenience store, and nobody's got a refrigerator within a hundred miles," Miani says.

"And he comes back with a pack of cold Guinness." Miani was amazed, and immediately asked the young man where on earth he'd found them.

"He said, 'Well, here's how we do it. We take the beer

and we bury it in a masonry jar in the ground. It's like fifty degrees colder down there than it is on the outside.'

"It wasn't refrigerated cold, but it sure as hell felt like it because it's hot as heck out there in the desert—but the beers were pretty cold," says Miani.

As for the Swiss NGO representative in the tent? "He'd been there eighteen months saving the world and really never actually talked to anyone," Miani says, incredulous.

The Swiss was motivated to drink beer. If he hadn't talked to the locals enough to find himself a cold one, then it seemed likely he hadn't talked to them about much else. Miani put two and two together and made a mental note of how credible a source the man would be when it came to other aspects of the local culture.

Keep an eye out for cues that point to the credibility and bias in your sources of information. When people talk, they sometimes throw out little reminders that the things they say represent their view on things. Little caveats or qualifiers, like, "In my opinion," "In my experience," or "From what I have read." If they don't, try to remind yourself that they're just one person, and that you might want to add the qualifiers in your own mind.

Like if your Colombian culture or language instructor says, "In South America, it's OK to be late. Punctuality is not a big deal and being late is not considered rude." If they don't say it themselves, you can tag on a silent "In your experience" in your mind.

They grew up in a specific region and had experience in certain settings, which might not apply in other contexts. For instance, they may or may not have worked in a professional context while they lived there, let alone one that relates to national security.

Being an informed consumer of information can also pay off when it comes to written sources. Take travel guides. You see them in the library, on racks in the bookstore, and on Amazon's virtual shelves. At first glance, most of them may not even really seem like they're targeted to you: *Wine and Dine Indonesia*, *Golfing in the South Pacific*. They usually give you a detached ten-thousand-foot view and seem like they might be great for planning a family vacation, but that's it.

Travel guides have saved Special Agent Sean Starnes serious headaches in Iraq and the dozen or so places he's worked in Southeast Asia. Starnes looks for a specific type of travel guide. One that gives him a street-level view.

"I don't like Frommer's much," Starnes says. "It tends to cater to people that are a little more affluent and a little more clueless. For me, they have to be guides written for backpackers, because backpackers are the people using bare-bones, streetwise information. Lonely Planet is good."

Starnes's most important criterion? The information can't be second or third hand. It needs to be from people who've been there. Robert Young Pelton is Starnes's favorite travel author. Pelton is a journalist and documentary filmmaker who has lived and reported from conflict zones most of his career.

"He wrote a book called *The World's Most Dangerous Places*. It's basically a backpacker's guide for thrill seekers. Everything you need to know about dangerous, crappy third-world places all over the world. Great book," says Starnes.

When you're reading about a culture, pay attention to who the author is. Where did they get their information from? Is it firsthand or based on research? Are they from the region themselves, or have they traveled there? How do those things affect the view they're presenting?

General information about a culture doesn't always, well, generalize. Any one source of information is likely to have some bias. This means that when it comes to working across cultures, you have to be a bit streetwise when it comes to your information.

Keep an eye out for cues to reliability. Question the information you're getting. Then, take the next step. Take action to mitigate bias, so you can gain a stronger foothold and be on firmer ground when you use cultural information to make calls that matter.

How do you do that? Shift to another vantage point. Find a different source to consult about the same topic. Get a fresh scoop that can give you an alternate view and perhaps a new way to think about the issue in question.

Say you're interested in history. If you've grown up reading and learning about world history from a Western perspective, your glasses are tinted a certain color, so to speak. You won't know how the Japanese experienced WWII, for example—how they think about it.

"There's more than one history in the world," General Zinni explains. "There are four basic histories. There's an Eastern history, a Middle Eastern history, a Western history, and there's an African history. There are subsets under that, but those are the four fundamental histories."

Zinni has made it a habit to read histories written by people in other parts of the world. Getting the local view on past events helps Zinni begin to understand why people elsewhere in the world look at things differently, why they don't necessarily believe the same things he, coming from a Western historical background, believes.

The very best history books, in Zinni's opinion, explain how history shaped the people the way they are today. What they think, believe, and care about today.

"A lot of historians don't do that," he says. But Tamim Ansary does, and that places his books among Zinni's top picks. "Ansary's book called *Destiny Disrupted*. Anybody who wants to understand the Middle East, I would recommend you read that first," he says.

To Zinni, the quest to overcome Western bias extends to all kinds of information. Not just history.

"You may learn language and you may learn customs. You can pick up a booklet that gives you those things. You're still coming from a Western perspective. The only way you succeed is to say, 'How do I place myself into that culture? How do I think like they do?'"

Zinni's solution? He looks for books that are written by people who are from the culture—people who can give him a different viewpoint and that can challenge the potential bias in the briefs and other information that's been produced for his consumption.

Once he's on the ground, he talks to people from all walks of life. He does this to gain yet another set of perspectives. Only then does he feel like he has a solid picture of what might really be going on.

It's best not to rely on any one fount of knowledge. Consulting with another source can give you a sense of whether your information generalizes or will hold up in the specific area or context you're headed into. It might also give you a whole new way to think about something you thought you already understood.

"Instead of lying prone when shooting at their enemies, they would exchange fire standing up. That's what we heard in our regional briefs about the Afghan warrior spirit. We learned that the mujahideen were extremely brave.

Like, absurdly brave," recalls US Air Force Captain Muñez.

"And what this guy was telling me didn't seem to fit with that."

Muñez was deployed as an intelligence collector with a provincial reconstruction team in Afghanistan. There was a very small market area in one of the villages, and Muñez spent most afternoons there speaking with the locals.

One afternoon he ended up sitting on the side of the street talking with an older man. Muñez knew that the average lifespan for an Afghan was shorter than many other places in the world. Living to be as old as this man appeared to be seemed rare.

So, he pointed to the man's beard and said, "You're a very wise man, how did you get to be so old and wise?"

The man's eyes widened, and he said, "Well, let's talk about that." Excitedly, the man told Muñez about his life.

He said that he was mujahideen when the Russians came and that he was part of a little elite bandit unit that jumped into the fray when people needed help. He had put together a small team of village men who would go out at night to destroy the Russian forces and do recon on the damage to their village. But, he said, no one knew that.

During the day he would get back to farming his land, tending his herd, and pretend to know little about fighting. At night though, it was a totally different story.

To Muñez, this running around in the shadows didn't

quite mesh with what he'd learned. So, he asked the old man why he was being secretive.

"When you think something is dead, you don't continue to kick it," the man explained.

In that moment, Muñez understood that this was in fact a clever strategy: If the enemy thinks that you're dumb, then why would they continue to waste their time with you? He realized that the way Americans think about what it means to be a warrior and a "hero" was different from how Afghans think about those things.

"We think that, with all our power and all our technology, that we're here to save the day. But they know how to manipulate, they know how to survive, and they know how to come together when they need to come together, even if it's in the middle of the night.

"And we don't realize that, because we have this expectation of what warrior culture is. We have that painted image in our mind where we say, are you wearing a suit? Do you go get dressed in the booth like Clark Kent and come out that superhero warrior that I expected?"

Talking to the old man helped Muñez clarify the Afghan concept of a "warrior." It also gave him a whole new frame for thinking about a lot of things related to Afghanistan. He no longer shares the impression that Afghans aren't warriors that some US servicemembers take home—an impression formed after they experience tardiness, lack of discipline, or slowness to adopt constructs related to logistics management.

"It all has to do with culture," says Muñez. "Personally, I don't see us having any more success than anybody else has had in Afghanistan. Except for the Afghans themselves."

Consulting another source and getting another perspective can give you better insight into the way people think about the world. It can also help you clarify local customs or rules. Senior Chief Petty Officer Vincent has spent nine of his many years with the Navy in Japan. From there, he's had numerous deployments all over the Western Pacific and to the Persian Gulf. The last two years, he and his family lived off-base.

"When we moved in, the following day the neighbor across the street, she brought us a gift. I can't remember if it was flowers or some food. It was kind of a welcome to our neighborhood."

Vincent and his wife were not sure what the appropriate response was. They had both grown up in the Philippines before coming to the US, and they were familiar with the script for gift giving in that country. But they weren't sure if there were different expectations in Japan. So, Vincent asked his Japanese landlord for advice.

"I went down and asked him, 'Hey, our neighbors across the street gave us a gift. I didn't respond right away.'

"He said, 'Yeah, that was good, they were just welcoming you.'"

Vincent explained to the landlord that in his experience in the Philippines, you respond back, usually within a few days.

"'How is it here?' I asked, and he said, 'It's up to you.'

"My wife and I thought it over. We gave them something American. I want to say cookies. In hindsight, I am sure they wouldn't have minded a bottle of whiskey," he says with a grin that melds into a chuckle.

"It became a never-ending, for almost a year, an exchange of gifts with these neighbors. They would bring something over, and we would turn around and give them something. Then they would turn around and give us something. I thought that was nice."

The exchange didn't go as expected. But the revolving gift exchange made Vincent and his wife feel welcome and connected to the community. More so than they had other times living abroad.

Maybe you've learned about the local customs, rules, and expectations from a class or book, or maybe from experience. Maybe you've lived or worked in a similar region and culture before, like Vincent—one that seems like it could be "close enough" that you might safely extrapolate some insights about how to engage. Even when you think you have a grasp on them, take an operational pause.

Check your understanding and clarify the local versions

of rules and customs. If your knowledge checks out, great. If there's a difference, the time you spent learning wasn't wasted. Even inaccurate knowledge can be a lifesaver when it alerts you to questions you might want to ask.

Think about all the learning and preparation you do before you land in a new culture as spooling up the engines of an F-16. If you don't get the turbine spun up in advance, you're bound to crash on takeoff. But, the real work, the real flying, the real fun begins when you're in the air.

Even if the things you learned ahead of time don't hold up to reality, spending the time to prep was still worthwhile. As Army Master Sergeant Carson puts it, "By reading before you go, even if it's wrong you have somewhere to start with. In fact, you'll know something's wrong, in most cases, quicker than you would otherwise."

When learning about a new culture, you can't take things at face value. Question whether the cultural information you come across is current, valuable, and correct. To check accuracy, try to consult with one or more alternative sources. These can be other written sources, or knowledgeable people.

Consider the trustworthiness of your sources to get a sense of their credibility and possible biases. Be on the lookout for sources that are likely to have a higher probability of accuracy, such as cultural insiders. Cultural insiders can be members or the culture or people who have firsthand experience living or working in the culture.

Pay attention to whether it seems a source is providing you opinions rather than facts or is making sweeping generalizations. If it seems they are, that's a cue to double-check using a different source. Keep your eyes peeled for inconsistencies. Make it a habit to look for information in more than one place. Keep checking, keep asking, and compare the answers you get.

Even so, at one time or another, your facts will be off. It's inevitable. You have to be ready to learn about the culture that's playing out right in front of you on the fly.

Key Points

- General facts and rules you learn about a culture won't always hold true

- Determine the credibility and biases of your cultural information providers

- Consult several sources with different viewpoints to obtain reliable cultural information

6

HOW TO LEARN MORE FROM
YOUR DAILY ENCOUNTERS

Never accept a misfire. When you learn to shoot, this lesson is likely drilled into you.

If you observe a misfire, do you chalk it up to a "bad round," and do nothing to investigate and fix the problem? That'd be making a mistake that could have severe consequences down the road.

It's the same when it comes to working across cultures. You're likely to have misfires every now and then. You're apt to find yourself in situations where things don't quite turn out as you planned. Often, you may feel that you'd be better off just moving on. Keep your life simple. Let it go.

Working in other cultures can sometimes feel like you're off-roading. You look in your rearview mirror, and all you see at first is a mud-splattered rear window. If you try to focus, you might start making out the outline of something unpleasant. Still, it often pays to hop out and get a clear view of what you've just rolled through.

Reflecting on your cultural encounters can help you draw out some important lessons about working effectively in that environment—considerations you can stick in your back pocket and use to do better and be safer in the future.

"I thought I was going to get stoned," says Major Moreau. While she was working as an attaché at the American embassy in Jordan, she also taught English to Jordanian senior officers. One day in class she had a real *Dang, I wish I hadn't done that* moment.

"I knew they were very sensitive. We are taught in school to never ask a man about how his wife is, or how his daughters are, or any female in their family. You stay away from females and female issues. But I thought it was OK for me, because I am a woman. I am not interested in anyone's wife."

On this particular day Moreau's headscarf had shifted slightly as she was talking in front of the class. "My students saw it immediately," she recalls. "They told me, 'Hey, fix your scarf, you can see a little part of your neck.' I said, 'Really?' So, I fixed it."

Next came the moment Moreau wishes she could take back; although in hindsight, it taught her some great lessons. The scarf episode had made her curious about something.

"I said, 'Do you mind if I ask you a question?'

"They were like, 'No, sure.'"

Moreau felt perfectly comfortable asking her question.

At this point she had developed a good relationship with the students. They called her their sister. They joked around with her, and they had been very open to all her questions about Islam. She had gotten the feeling they enjoyed teaching her about their religion.

"So, I said, 'Why is it in some Arab countries, like in the Gulf countries, you can see a woman's neck, and here you can't?'"

The answer came immediately and forcefully. Several of the students were speaking over each other. "They were telling me, 'They have it wrong. They don't read the Quran properly.'"

Moreau, still curious, pushed further. "I said, 'A neck is a neck. I can't distinguish a woman's neck from a man's neck. They look the same to me.'"

The tension in the room rose to a boiling point. "Absolutely not!" was the booming consensus. "'A woman's neck is sexy, it is provocative, and a man's neck is not,' they said. They were extremely upset," recalls Moreau.

Moreau found herself in the middle of a toxic debate. She realized she had to extract herself. So, she quickly changed the topic and was relieved when she managed to get the students refocused on the lesson.

Moreau didn't understand why talking about women's necks was so sensitive for them. It was a shock for her that, even as a woman, she couldn't ask about this. Especially since all her other discussions with the group about religion had been so open.

Thinking back to the experience later, she came to a realization. "I think all my other questions about Islam had nothing to do with sexuality. And the neck is sexy, or is somehow linked to sexuality, or sex. And that made it very inappropriate."

In retrospect, she also thought it was possible that the fact that she was an outsider made asking these questions worse. Maybe her questions appeared to be challenging their views. Maybe they felt she was questioning their ideology and their religion.

She also wondered whether the response would have been different if she had asked the question of each student individually and in private—outside the context of needing to defend their religion in public. Moreau wanted to pretend this incident hadn't happened. Instead, she thought about what had gone wrong. She dissected it, and she learned from it.

You put your foot in your mouth. We all do it. What do you do when it happens? Gloss it over? Move on? When you goof up, it can be tempting to pretend it never happened. Blunders are embarrassing and unpleasant to think about. They're reminders that we're not perfect. Mistakes you make in engagements with foreigners can seem deceptively easy to write off. Was it even a mistake?

Thinking back on it, they were probably the ones who were unreasonable. Or crazy.

Often, it seems that moving on is all you have time for anyway. But, every time you do, you miss out. You pass the opportunity to learn something new, and you increase the chances of making the same mistake again. When things go south, dwelling for a moment on what went wrong is an excellent way to learn. The cross-cultural SMEs made this a habit; part of their routine. It helped them come up with questions to learn more about the culture.

For example, Moreau generated three: Would it have been different if a man had asked the same question? Would these male students have been able to discuss this topic peacefully if she hadn't been there? Could she have asked them in private and received a less explosive response? She had several months left on her assignment and lots of time to find the answers.

Sometimes when you think back on an interaction, you may realize there's a pattern. Your slipup is one you may have made before. Suddenly you're able to draw out a general principle that will help you avoid making the same mistake in the future.

Lieutenant Colonel Matthew Smith was studying at the Russian Combined Arms Academy as part of his foreign area officer training program. A number of international officers were also attending the school. Among them was a

Syrian colonel. Smith's room was right next to the colonel's, and they interacted regularly.

"We had built pretty good rapport, and I thought we had a pretty good relationship. We were just acquaintances. But we talked in a fairly free manner," Smith recalls.

One evening there was a retirement party for an instructor. Smith was having a side conversation with the Syrian colonel. They had been discussing day-to-day life at the school—harmless stuff—when suddenly the colonel changed topics. "'I wonder what is going to happen with the situation in Iran,' he said," Smith recalls.

There had been a lot of discussion in the news at the time about Iran and nuclear weapons. The US and Israel were in the spotlight.

Smith jumped in. "I said something to effect that it was a bit of a dangerous situation."

Seeing the colonel's reaction, he regretted it instantly. "We only talked once a week, but it was quite clear with verbal cues and his actions following that he felt insulted. I realized that I had probably overestimated our rapport."

Smith wasn't sure what the colonel's view on Iran was, but imagined that overall, he probably thought Iran was doing a good thing—that the country was being helpful with Israel, from the Syrian perspective.

Their interaction decreased quite a bit after that. The colonel stopped seeking Smith out to converse and ask questions. Smith thinks that maybe the colonel reacted this way not because of what he said, but how he said it.

"I think it was also the aspect that I cut him off. I should have thought before I spoke. I just went ahead and said what I thought about it. I could have instead let him get his view across. This is what I think he was after. A lot of times, people just want you to hear what they have to say."

He also wonders whether the age and rank difference between them could have been a factor. "My American way is to speak freely. He was a little bit older than me. Perhaps in his culture he expected me to listen because he was more senior in rank. And I didn't really give him that opportunity."

Regardless of the reason, Smith's take-home message was clear. As he puts it, "It was a lesson point for me. Do more listening and less talking."

Smith says this lesson kicked in multiple times later in his career. In Russia and other places, when he was asked about US policy or how the US views something, he would pause and think to himself: "Perhaps I don't need to come right out and say 'This is the way I see it.'"

Getting in a cycle of learning from your mistakes may seem difficult and unpleasant at first. After some practice, it gets easier. Working on a simple habit can help you benefit from your mistakes and improve your future interactions. Ask for feedback.

Part of what makes intercultural blunders unpleasant is

that they're public. There's always at least one other person present. You can turn this to your advantage. After an awkward interaction, find someone who can give a different perspective on what happened—someone who can give you some insight and help improve your cultural skills and knowledge.

Air Force Colonel Bruce Bennett spent three years in Colombia on an assignment.

"When I had just gotten to Colombia, I was invited to a meeting," he recalls. "They put me in a place of honor at the end of the table. I thought I was just going to listen to the agenda. But I had a lot of difficulty even understanding, listening at that time."

Bennet thought he'd focus on his comprehension. He soon learned that his hosts had different plans.

"The next thing I realize, this colonel friend of mine, quote 'friend,' was introducing me to stand up and speak in front of this audience," Bennett recalls whispering an expletive under his breath.

"I knew my Spanish wasn't good at that time. I mean, I had to actually think and then translate, think and translate, and my vocabulary was now on the line. I was in front of their air force, military, security force." Bennett was eager to make a good impression.

"I stood up and I said, 'I apologize. I'm a little worried. I'm embarrassed for my poor Spanish.' And they all laughed. They all laughed pretty hard. And I realized that I probably said something wrong, but I didn't know what."

Bennett moved on, but kept that thought in the back of his mind. At the end of the day, the colonel who had put him on stage came to see him, still with a smirk on his face.

"He said, 'That was really funny.' And I go, 'What did I say? I thought I had said I was embarrassed.' He said, 'You said you were pregnant.'"

The colonel clarified that the Spanish word for embarrassed is *avergonzado*.

"I'd heard of *embarrazado*," Bennett explains. "So that was the word that came to my mind. You know, I'm standing up under pressure and I can't think of embarrassed. So, I fall back on Spanglish, embarrazado. Well it turns out you can only be embarrazada." In Spanish, feminine words end with an *a*, masculine words with an *o*.

Bennett laughs good-naturedly and puts the comment in context. "I had a little belly at the time. I could probably pass it off better now. But I told them that I was pregnant." He chuckles, amused that the key word here was embarrassed. That he certainly was. But he learned from the experience.

Getting feedback can help you learn from your mistakes. It can also let you know when you're on the right track when the situation is unclear. That's what Kovach, a retired Army Ranger, did when he was working as a contractor in

Iraq. Kovach has lived and worked all over the world. Europe, Korea, Japan, Central America. Most recently he spent six years in Iraq advising the Iraqi Army on how to conduct training.

"We had just sold military equipment to them. My team tried to set them up like the US military in regard to training, so they could learn how to use the equipment and fight with it," he says.

After each training event Kovach's trainers assessed the Iraqi soldiers' performance. Kovach passed the results up the chain to the two- and three-star generals in charge of the units, outlining the strengths, and the weaknesses.

"I remember seeing on the three-star's face kind of a look of shock that I would even talk about that," says Kovach. The general was reacting to Kovach's reporting on the areas the units still needed to work on. "It was the look of 'Man, I can't believe you are talking about that.'"

Kovach had made it a habit after every meeting to ask his interpreter for feedback. "I wanted to make sure I wasn't doing anything that would offend them," he says. When he asked about the shocked look on the general's face the interpreter shrugged.

"He said, 'No, you are doing everything right, and you need to continue. It's just that Arabs don't like to hear bad news,'" Kovach recalls.

He trusted his interpreter, so he pressed on. About three

or four months in, the general couldn't contain himself any longer.

After receiving yet another report on his units' weaknesses, Kovach reports that he burst out, "You always start off with bad things. I don't want to know bad things."

"I felt that we had made a lot of progress in the fact that he could tell me that," Kovach explains. "It showed that there was a relationship there. If they don't trust you, they are just going to nod back and forth and be glad when you're leaving."

He told the general that if he didn't share that information, then he wasn't doing his job. He explained that by knowing the strengths and weaknesses, the units would know what to work on when they went back to their divisions.

The general nodded. "He said, 'Ah, that makes sense.' And a couple of times when we sat down after that he said, 'Ok, start with the bad stuff.'"

Kovach had asked for feedback from his interpreter. In this case the verdict was positive. He was doing well. He didn't need to adjust. If he hadn't asked, he may have felt uncomfortable continuing to deliver the bad news.

Keep an eye on people's reactions to you. Try to gauge the effect you have on them. Find someone who can give you an inside perspective, and an honest opinion about how you did. Sometimes you'll get a thumbs-up, other times a thumbs-down. Adjust accordingly.

What if you don't have repeated interactions with the same people? Or if you're not even spending all that much time in one place? It can seem like each experience is a one-off, with its own unique lesson—lessons that will never apply again. How can dwelling on your past experiences help you long-term, when you're jumping from one seemingly exceptional situation to the next?

When you think back on your experiences, make it a deliberate point to look for commonalities and connections between situations. Think about similarities and differences between groups of people or cultures you come across. Finding common threads and making them explicit in your mind can help you identify lessons that generalize. And making a connection to a past experience can sometimes help you solve a current problem.

Air Force Master Sergeant Reynolds was a tactical air controller on assignment in Korea. He was in the middle of a joint air-to-ground training exercise. He'd given both the American and Korean pilots their targets. The birds were in the air.

A little while into the exercise he realized that he was only getting call-backs from the American pilots. The Korean flight training code was the same as the US. Call-backs were SOP and mandatory. What was going on?

Reynolds called out to one of the American pilots. He

confirmed that the Koreans had engaged their targets. Reynolds's impression of the Korean pilots took an instant nosedive. Where he came from, if you don't follow procedure, it's because you're incompetent. Reynolds walked away upset about the Koreans' failure to follow protocol. Then, he thought about it some more and made a connection.

After the exercise, he thought back to the days when he taught at the Korean Air-Ground Operations School. Some of the students he called on to answer a question or take part in a role-playing exercise would just sit there, silent. They wouldn't say a word. After a while he discovered that their English skills were not up to their own standards, so they were embarrassed to speak up in class.

"Could that be what was going on here?" he asked himself. It was possible. Reynolds applied an insight he'd had while working with Koreans in the schoolhouse years earlier to the Korean pilots he was currently working with. Doing that gave him a starting point for understanding the situation better.

Even with experiences that take place in very different parts of the world, it can still pay off to look for similarities and connections. Sometimes you can find lessons that transcend hemispheres. Air Force Colonel Rodriguez grew up in Peru. When he found himself ten thousand miles away in Afghanistan walking from a NATO headquarters to an American airbase, he ran across a situation that reminded him of something he'd seen in his youth.

"There was a kid that was always annoying, and I am talking about maybe nine- to twelve-year-old kids, and their command of the English language is amazing. They knew words like *my friend, you're my friend.* One of the things they do is try to sell things.

"And this major that was walking with me, the kid was trying to sell him this thing. It was one of these bracelets, but he kept saying 'No, no, no.'

"Finally, the kid said, 'You're my friend. This is for you. For free.'"

This scene immediately triggered a memory in Rodriguez's mind. "I was maybe fourteen or fifteen years old. I was walking downtown Peru one time and there was like five kids come up to me that wanted money," he recalls.

"Growing up in South America, in a third-world country, you are used to seeing very poor conditions, and it's not uncommon to get the poor kids come up to you and ask for money. They're often working for either some adult or for their family. And I would usually give them maybe a sol back then. It's like a dollar here.

"But this time, there were like five kids that wanted money. So, I said, 'I tell you what, I will just buy you ice cream.' So, we all went to the store and I bought ice cream for these little kids.

"Well, believe it or not, a week later I was in the same

spot, and I see the same kids. But this time, it's not only them, but they brought their friends. So now I found myself in a pickle. How do I deal with this? Now I'm feeding a bunch of kids.

"That was a lesson learned. Giving is good but giving within the circumstances that you are in, the environment that you are in, can sometimes get you in trouble. So that was a lesson for me at fourteen or fifteen years old."

As the ice cream scene flashed through his mind, Rodriguez gave the major some advice. "I told him, 'Don't take it, don't take it.'"

The major didn't listen. "And he was like, 'No, it's a nice offer.' So, he took it.

"And I said, 'OK, you are going to find out what will happen. I knew that this kid was trying to build trust, and the thing he was saying was, now you owe me something at a later time.

"Two weeks later, we are walking and here comes this kid, and he remembers. He tells the major, 'You got this for free and now you buy.' And now he is forced to buy to keep that good relationship with the kid."

Your mind is wired to make connections. You're apt to automatically start noticing things that are similar and things that are different in the cultures you work in. Seize those moments. Dwell on them and explore them. Try to draw some meaning out of them by looking for commonalities and differences between groups. Extract the essence. A takeaway or lesson you can take with you wherever you're headed next.

You can look for trends in people's behavior, like Rodriguez did. Noticing common patterns might help you interpret things that are going on around you in new environments. You can also look for ways to bring your cultural skills to new areas.

Reflecting on his experiences in disparate places like Colombia, Japan, and Bulgaria has helped Colonel Bennett develop a strategy. Wherever it's possible for him to meld into the human landscape, he actively takes steps to blend in. He does his best to become a chameleon.

"In Colombia, I developed a capability to adopt the mannerisms and characteristics of the group of people that I was working with, and kind of camouflage myself in the community.

"I think a lot of times I was able to blend in walking down the street as a Colombian as opposed to a foreigner, and, I had several people accuse me of being a Colombian on the telephone because I used the mannerisms and things like that, and I picked up their accent." For Bennett, this meant making some changes to his usual way of being around people.

"I had to do things that I don't normally do," he says. "I'm not very sociable, I'm not very outgoing, but in Colombia you have to be social and outgoing. You have to compliment women on their appearance when you first meet them. You have to give the formal kiss of greeting, either one or two cheeks, and that's something that in America we're not very comfortable with. I adapted to that style."

And this became a general strategy for fitting into new places.

"What I learned in Colombia—I applied some of the same skills in Bulgaria and they worked," he says. "Colombia and Bulgaria have a different style. But they each had a style and I adopted that. I was accosted, if you will, by Bulgarians asking me for directions because they thought I was a Bulgarian. So, I learned a key word or a phrase or two that said, 'I'm sorry. I don't speak Bulgarian. I'm just a crazy American.'"

Over the course, he found that his "chameleon strategy" wouldn't always apply. When he works in regions where his physical appearance is drastically different from the locals, he plays defense. "It's hard to hide the fact that you're a Westerner in Japan, so there I focused on doing things that wouldn't piss off the people, if you will."

Look across your experiences in different places and try to find some common threads in how people think and act and the best ways to get work done. Or, see if you can put your finger on features that seem to vary from place to place. Find your takeaways.

Make sure you hit the pause button every now and then to notice what's going on around you. Be deliberate about learning from your experiences and your mistakes when you're working across cultures. Because mistakes will happen. You're bound to have engagements that could have gone better had you known a little more. It happens to everybody.

When the tempo is high, and the pressure is on to keep moving, it's tempting to explain away your hiccups, to dismiss odd slipups as one-off occurrences, or get bogged down placing blame. *It wasn't me. It was them.*

Avoid these traps. It doesn't get you anywhere. Instead, when there's time, reach out and ask for feedback. Reflect and extract the lesson once the tempo slows down. Dwell a little longer on things that went wrong.

You won't get a huge mind-altering insight every time. You might just learn a little trick or tidbit you didn't know before. Every lesson, no matter how small, makes you quicker, smarter, and more flexible.

Key Points

- Reflecting on your intercultural encounters builds your cultural understanding

- Ask for feedback after awkward interactions to improve future performance

- Compare across cultural experiences to draw general lessons

7

HOW TO HANDLE PUZZLING BEHAVIOR

Working across cultures is a bit like diving in extremely murky water. It doesn't seem to matter what kind of light source you bring. You're not a great deal better off whether you jump in equipped with a Sea Elite Mini or wielding a high-lumen dive torch. Either way, you can't see much past the reach of your hand. Why? Because all the little particles in the water reflect the light back at you.

It's the same when you're working with people from other cultures. Whether you go in with a set of simple do's and don'ts in your back pocket, armed with a degree in cross-cultural studies, or with thirty years of overseas work under your belt, things are going to come—out of nowhere—at you that you couldn't have seen in advance.

People are going to react in unexpected ways to the things you say and do, to the way you look, move, and talk, and to circumstances and events you have no control over. People's behaviors will inevitably be echoes of a myriad of things you can't see.

This has been Marine Corps Lieutenant Colonel Lund's experience. "You can't possibly cover every possible contingency that could arise from cultural interactions. There will always be surprises," he says with emphasis, "and the challenge is to not be thrown off pace by them."

How do you avoid losing your footing when the unexpected happens?

When you dive in murky water, you remain ready to make sense of things as they come into your small sphere of awareness. As they float into your hand, bump into your leg, or wrap themselves around your mask.

The same applies when you're working across cultures. Count on being surprised. Stay prepared to make sense of things as they come at you. Assuming this posture will help you cast the prep you do in advance in an appropriate light. Don't expect that it will fully prevent you from being surprised. That's unrealistic. Instead, think of the courses you take and preparation you do as starting points.

As Army Staff Sergeant Aaronson puts it, "It prevents some surprises, but it's not going to prevent all of them. It gives me a good baseline."

Army Captain Firestone has come to the same conclusion: "Training courses don't give you the perfect answer to everything. They give you the answers for some things, and that will help you figure out answers for other things, so you can adapt."

Courses and prep give you starting points for figuring things out. Going in with this mindset will help you turn some attention toward honing the skill that is truly valuable when uncertainty strikes. As Marine Gunnery Sergeant Chapman puts it, "You should expect surprises to happen, and learn how to handle them."

When you're working across cultures, the people around you aren't coming from the same place you are. Literally and figuratively. Their values, beliefs, and norms are different from yours, and they sometimes have different motivations and intentions behind the things they do and say than you might expect. Things are less likely to be what they seem in your interactions with foreigners than they are when you're dealing with someone from your own culture.

Your first impressions are more likely to be a distortion of what's really going on. You can't just lean back, let your hair down, and hit cruise control. You have to stay on the lookout for situations where your first impressions might be warped. To do that, watch out for behaviors, events, or situations that don't fit your expectations—things that don't seem like business as usual, or that just don't sit right with you.

Marine Corps Lieutenant Colonel Russell Jamison spent eight months in Iraq as an advisor to an Iraqi infantry brigade. When he arrived, his unit was replacing another team of Marines. They all had a meeting to introduce them to their Iraqi counterparts. Jamison remembers this first staff meeting vividly.

"There were many friendly faces on that Iraqi staff," he recalls. "Except the deputy, Colonel Khoury. He sat the entire time with his arms crossed, a frown on his face. He would not give me eye contact at all." Colonel Khoury was clearly angry.

After the meeting Jamison approached the lieutenant colonel he was replacing. "I asked him 'OK, what's the problem with Colonel Khoury?'

And he said, 'He just hates Americans.' And he left it at that."

Over the next few days this story started rubbing Jamison the wrong way. It seemed to him like there was more to it.

He recruited a major to help him look into the matter. The two asked around. They uncovered some interesting details surrounding the history of the outgoing team's interactions with the Iraqi brigade, and with the colonel in particular.

Jamison discovered that as a lieutenant, Colonel Khoury had served five years on the front lines in the Iran-Iraq war. He had parachuted into Kuwait during the Iraqi invasion of Kuwait in 1990. He had been shot there twice with a US Army 5.56 mm rifle, and he had fought in Operation Iraqi Freedom.

"So, the man had extensive and complete infantry experience, to include parachute operations," Jamison explains with appreciation.

The brigade was going through basic training. "They had developed a training package, to get them ready to be used in the counterinsurgency fight," he says. As part of the basic training, most of the Iraqis were given classes on operating and maintaining the AK-47 rifle. Before Jamison arrived Colonel Khoury had tried to excuse himself from this training.

"My predecessor essentially told him, and I am going to use coarse language here—please excuse me—he told him to sit down and shut the F up and go to class."

Jamison was incredulous. The idea that a man with five years of combat experience in Kuwait and in OIF needed training on the AK-47 was ridiculous and insulting.

"If I was sitting in his seat, and I had some punk from another nation, who didn't even have close to the combat experience, had told me to sit down and shut the F up? I would have probably despised anyone wearing that uniform as well," Jamison reflects.

It took Jamison the better part of three weeks to dig himself out of that hole. To show Colonel Khoury that his team was there to assist him and be part of the solution—not to disparage and insult him. Jamison didn't accept the explanation that the colonel "just hates Americans." It seemed to him that there was likely more to the story. He investigated the situation thoroughly to find out why.

When you're operating in a foreign environment, you have to be ready to dig deeper into the little mysteries that present themselves to you. You're dealing with new people, who come from different backgrounds. There's a lot of room for misunderstandings to arise and fester. You want to make sure you're working with information that can inform good decisions.

The first step is to stay on your toes and keep alert even to minor things that seem off or different about people's behavior. Don't write them off. Treat little inconsistencies or wrinkles in the fabric of your otherwise seemingly smooth readings of your situation as opportunities. Take them as openings for you to step in and get beyond the way things appear at first glance. You'll never find out what's beneath a surface if you don't scratch it. You've got to dig into puzzling interactions or anomalous behavior to find real answers.

Secondly, try to take an open-ended approach to your inquiry. If you let your first impression determine the information you look for, you're less likely to learn anything useful. Say you asked your interpreter the following question: "Does General Khouri hate Americans?" They'd probably say, "Yes."

Now consider that you instead asked, "Why did General

Khoury look angry and upset in the meeting?" Asking open-ended questions like, "Why?" sets you up to get meatier answers—ones that get you closer to what might really be going on.

Lieutenant Colonel Rudy Atallah is a retired Air Force foreign area officer who now consults with international companies. For one project, he had been hired by an oil company to deliver a risk management and leadership training course on a rig where Egyptian and American roughnecks were working side by side.

As he was teaching them how to work with each other, a problem surfaced. "They had one Egyptian guy on the deck, Abasi, who had been getting very short-tempered and was yelling at the other Egyptians." Atallah discovered that the leadership was getting ready to fire Abasi. Nobody wanted to work with him anymore.

Apparently, the man used to be a phenomenal worker. Now he wasn't. This grabbed Atallah's interest.

"Have you asked yourselves the question why he's acting this way?" he asked the leadership. "Have you sat down and talked to him?"

"No, he's just acting belligerent," they said. Atallah was suspicious. There had to be more to the story. So, he sat down with Abasi at dinner.

"I said, 'So how's it going, how's life treating you?'

"And he said, 'Difficult. These people don't listen to

me.'" Abasi went on to complain about the other people on the rig.

Atallah changed tack to get beyond the obvious. He asked Abasi how his family was doing. The man immediately hung his head, and Atallah knew he was getting warmer.

"I said, 'Well, what's wrong?' And he said nothing. So, I said, 'How's your wife?'"

Abasi shook his head and made a choked-up sound. It turned out his wife was in the hospital. She needed a kidney, and he didn't have the money to pay for it.

The pieces were coming together, but Atallah still wasn't sure how exactly this explained the man's behavior at work.

"I said 'Well, how's work going?'

"He goes, 'It's terrible.'

"I said, 'Well, why do you keep yelling at everybody?'"

Abasi then explained that he had been promised a senior position and it hadn't come through yet. He was getting impatient for the promotion because he wanted to be able to make more money so he could pay for the kidney for his wife.

Now, Abasi's behavior made sense. "This is an Arab mentality. Being too proud to ask for help," Atallah explains. "It shows weakness. The man of the house is supposed to step up and fix problems. And he was trying to do that, but he was beyond his capacity to do anything. Fifteen thousand dollars is a lot of money for somebody signing for barely fifteen hundred a month.

"He clearly loved his wife and he wanted to make sure that she was OK. So, he was lashing out at everybody, hoping that they would do better work, so it would make him look better so he would get promoted. But he was going about it the wrong way."

Atallah told Abasi there might be another way. He talked to the leadership and told them the man's story. They immediately organized a donation on the rig, and enough money was raised for a kidney transplant.

"I talked to him about all this alone, so he didn't feel embarrassed in front of everybody," Atallah says. "So he didn't feel belittled or emasculated in any way. Also, I never told him, 'This is where you screwed up.'"

He never lectured Abasi on what he should have done differently. Still, Atallah feels confident that Abasi walked away with a different understanding of how he should work.

"It was clear to him. Even people that he had been pretty rough on, they started donating money—what little money they had. And that blew him away. I know he was thinking, 'My god, I can't believe I've been treating them like dirt. I've been acting like an ass.' He didn't say it, but you could see his brain was just—the wheels were turning and things, clue lights were just coming on and he just started to cry."

Atallah dug into Abasi's situation in an open-ended way.

This helped him understand why the man was acting the way he was, and this helped Atallah figure out how the company could turn the man's negative, destructive behavior around. When Abasi got back after tending to his wife, he turned out to be the company's best worker.

Be on the lookout for things that don't make sense. Keep alert even to minor things that seem off or different. Don't write them off. They're likely signs that it's time to have an extra think about what's going on around you. Ask "Why?" and other open-ended questions. Seek information to disentangle puzzling interactions and weird behaviors. Mentally prepare yourself that sometimes you might have to ask more than once, and possibly in a couple of different ways.

Air Force Colonel Kurt Marisa was working in Suriname as a defense attaché when a conflict erupted between Suriname and Guyana. The border between the two regions is located someplace deep in the jungle. No one knows exactly where. Some think it is marked by a certain river. However, in one location the river splits in two different directions. It has never been decided which of those splits is the river that marks the border. The result? A disputed tribal region.

"When this crisis flared up, both sides were sending forces to the border," Marisa explains. "The Guyanese had troops down there that possibly were going into Suriname proper." The deputy chief of mission asked Marisa to go into the region to see if he could find out why tensions had suddenly erupted.

Marisa and a small team of embassy officials and translators hired a bush plane. They talked to the Surinamese and Guyanese troops they encountered along the way and eventually ended up near a Surinamese Amerindian tribal village. The chief agreed to speak with them. "At first he went into a long diatribe against the Guyanese, and how much they bothered him," Marisa remembers.

The conversation was interesting, to say the least—even the logistics of it. It took place in three languages. After a cumbersome forty-five minutes of back and forth, Marisa started seeing inconsistencies in the chief's story about their motivations for keeping the conflict going.

"What he said they had done stopped making sense," Marisa says, and explains that he went over the events several times. Asking the same questions in different ways. What was the chief upset about? What had the Guyanese done? What had started the conflict?

"I was letting him see my perplexity so he would understand and want to better explain himself. This is an elicitation technique of 'Please help me understand this better, because I am just not understanding it and not that knowledgeable about it.'

"Eventually he instead started complaining about the

Surinamese government ignoring his village and not giving them adequate benefits and support," Marisa says. He had a sense they'd reached the bottom line.

Out of nowhere, the chief suddenly laid it out. He had made up the story that the Guyanese were challenging the border. He was trying to get attention from the Surinamese government, so he could get them to meet his repeated requests for resources and support for his tribe.

"It finally came out that he had basically manufactured a whole border conflict to garner attention from the government, so he could ask for resources," Marisa says with amazement. "His confession surprised me. I had suspected that the crisis was really much ado about nothing. But I wasn't prepared for the frankness of 'I made it up just to get the government's attention.'"

Marisa asked the chief if he didn't think this would destroy his credibility with the Surinamese government.

The answer was no. "He said, 'It's not lying if it gets resources and benefits for my people.'"

Marisa reported his findings to the Ministry of Defense. They stood down military activities along the border. But they didn't fight with the chief. Instead, the tribal group ended up getting many of the things they requested.

"The government needed them as a counter-balance to the African tribal groups in the jungle," Marisa explains.

Marisa's discovery of the chief's true intentions didn't

come about easily. Sometimes people have no problem revealing their true thoughts, motives, or intentions. All you have to do is ask. Other times, you might be able to tease them out with some finesse. By coming at topics from another angle and asking the same question in different ways. Circling in on the issue like a hawk.

When you're working with people from your own culture, you might get away with putting your brain on autopilot now and again. Lean back and rely on comforting thoughts like, "When people say X, it usually means Y," and, "When people behave a certain way, we can all agree about what that means." Like when someone says something that isn't a true representation of reality, then we tend to agree they're lying, and lying is bad.

The thing is, as Colonel Marisa discovered when he dug deeper, not everyone sees things this way. You can't simply write off their way of thinking in favor of your own. The people you're dealing with are important to your mission. The relationships are key.

When you're working in other cultures, people constantly say and do things you might feel like you just don't understand. Resist the impulse to write them off. It's quick and easy to think "Hey, that's just them, it's their personality," or "They're just incompetent." Yet, if you pause for a moment, you may get a sneaking feeling there's more to the story and that if you knew what it was, you'd have a better grip on the situation.

Behaviors that seem strange or suspicious may stem from cultural differences in what people know, believe, and value. Attempting to make sense of the oddities can help you gain a deeper understanding of the culture you're in. Keeping one simple question in mind can illuminate a good path through the fog of confusion: "Is there some cultural difference at work here?"

Marine Corps Colonel Len DeFrancisci was a major when he did a threat assessment in a remote valley region in Afghanistan. The memory is clear in his mind because it entailed an engagement that temporarily threw him for a loop.

As part of doing his assessment, he sat down with a local elder. He talked about the weather, he talked about the crops, and he drank tea. He finally got to the ask. Was there a location his team could camp out while they monitored activity in the area?

The elder shook his head vigorously. No, no, no. If he was seen to cooperate, then the village would start receiving night letters from the Taliban again.

This piqued DeFrancisci's interest. "When did you receive night letters?" he asked.

The Afghan elder rocked back and forth as he picked away at the frilly ends of the rug underneath him. "A while ago," he replied softly, shaking his head. His vague response hung in the air.

DeFrancisci was a bit perplexed. Something didn't jibe. Why didn't the elder just tell him when the letters had arrived? He kept probing. But no matter what angle he tried he couldn't pin down a specific time. A stray thought then entered DeFrancisci's mind. He'd never seen a calendar in any of the Afghan homes he'd been into.

"Maybe they just don't think about time the same way I do," he thought to himself. He considered that some cultural difference might be in play.

He changed his approach. He asked the elder how many times the village had planted crops since the letters arrived. Then, he worked out the answer in his own terms. About two years. DeFrancisci realized that this was as precise an answer as he could expect. To the elder it felt like it had just happened. This is how strong the Taliban's stronghold of fear was on the village.

DeFrancisci could have easily written off the man's seemingly elusive answers to "shadiness." He didn't. Instead he did a bit of digging. He asked himself whether the elder's strange behavior might be attributed to a cultural difference.

Just like a metal detector can be tuned to detect different types of metal, your people-sensors are naturally calibrated too. You're programmed to interpret what people say and do in ways that make perfect sense within your own culture. You do it quickly, effortlessly, and automatically. That means that when you're in another culture, your first insights may be a result of miscalibration.

Imagine this. You're overseeing a series of humanitarian aid missions in Bangladesh. Numerous remote villages along the coast have been devastated by a record-breaking cyclone. In just three days you have successfully coordinated the delivery of supplies to many affected areas.

You're in your hotel room. Your head is spinning. You're exhausted, but relieved. Pulling off the transportation logistics was a nightmare. The local infrastructure was crappy before the storm. Its current state is easily pre-Stone Age. Your TV is droning in the background. An image on the screen jerks you to attention. It's the village you visited this morning. You personally oversaw delivery and distribution in this location.

An outraged reporter gestures dramatically toward the devastation behind her and exclaims, "The situation here appears utterly hopeless." She sticks the microphone in the face of an old man sitting on a pile of debris.

The man weaves back and forth and croaks in broken English, "I haven't had a meal in three days."

Marine Corps Colonel Riker, who experienced this firsthand, was annoyed when the story ran on TV. He took a deep breath and called one of the local embassy reps. He asked them why people were saying they hadn't eaten. After a fair bit of probing, Riker discovered that in Bangladesh, if you don't have rice, then it is considered that you haven't had a meal. The man on TV didn't mean that he hadn't eaten in three days. All he was saying was that he hadn't had rice.

"That was an eye opener," Riker reflects. "I thought I was pretty savvy about different cultures and everything, but that was totally the first time I'd heard this. So that kind of nuance in the language, and what people say and how it translates I think is very important."

Colonel Riker has worked in a few places over his career. Okinawa, Korea, Philippines, Cuba, Saudi Arabia, Kuwait, Iraq, Egypt, Pakistan, Bangladesh, Myanmar. Oh, and Norway. He still found himself taken aback in this situation. By checking into it, he found out something new about the culture.

When you're dealing with a foreigner whose actions seem off at first blush, be sure you check behind the curtain. Ask open-ended questions to get information that can help you disentangle the mystery. Give some latitude and consider that maybe they're acting "weird" because of their culture. Otherwise, you'll miss opportunities to find out what's really going on.

Asking if a behavior is cultural isn't the end of the process. It's simply a hint to yourself. A prompt to recognize that your first interpretation of a situation is merely a guess, and to explore the puzzling interaction a little more.

Say you think to yourself, "Could this have something to do with culture?" Having this thought might inspire you to run this scenario by a cultural insider, and in the course of doing this you might discover that people sometimes do, say, and want things for reasons you'd never have dreamt of yourself.

Key Points

- Expect to be surprised when working across cultures

- Ask "why" to disentangle weird behavior and puzzling interactions

- Look into culture as a potential source of seemingly odd behavior

8

FIGURING OUT WHY
PEOPLE DO WHAT THEY DO

"They seemed stubborn. That was my first thought. All I kept hearing was, 'We don't need any help. We are working things out ourselves.'" USMC Foreign Area Officer Major Paul Sotomayor had found himself in a jungle of confusion in Panama.

Sotomayor was tasked with conducting a capabilities assessment of the Panamanian National Aeronaval Service, a service branch of the Panamanian Public Forces. The US embassy had earmarked funds to help improve the unit. It was Sotomayor's job to figure out how those resources would be best spent. At first it had looked like the job would be a piece of cake.

Sotomayor had visited the unit a couple of months prior to coming down for the assessment itself. During these visits he had made great inroads with the colonel he would be coordinating with. They went out to dinner and had several good conversations.

"He had just come back from living in the US for eight months, attending school, and he was just very positive about the experience. He really liked those little Raisinettes. 'I can't find them here anywhere,' he said. So, I picked up a box of them for him," Sotomayor remembers. The two even negotiated a senior leadership training course aimed at the unit's senior enlisted and junior officers to take place simultaneously with the assessment.

But when he returned to conduct the assessment the colonel had been replaced, and a new one put in his place. The new colonel stonewalled.

"He basically was like, 'I have no clue what you guys are doing here, and we are too busy to entertain you,'" Sotomayor remembers.

Over the next several days, Sotomayor tried repeatedly to connect with the local leadership, to no avail.

"I have hit thirteen countries in the region, and seven or eight focused on assessments, and never have I had anyone be this standoffish," Sotomayor marvels. "There was a lot of money that could have gone to supporting these guys, and they knew it. They just didn't want it."

At first blush, the Panamanians' aloofness seemed irrational to Sotomayor. After some careful consideration, though, he found that maybe it wasn't so simple. He took time to brainstorm other possible reasons they might have for putting him off. Sotomayor realized that there were possibly several other factors at play.

"Well, they were just invaded by us twenty years ago," he says. "I would drum up that being part of it. Those junior officers during the US invasion are now the leaders running the national security forces of Panama."

In addition, the right relationships may not have been in place—on several fronts. Sotomayor had built personal rapport with one individual. But when he came for the assessment he had to start over with the new personnel, and at that time the window of opportunity for relationship building had closed.

"At that point, it was a lot harder, you know, because we didn't have that informal setting to just chat and get to know each other," he reflects.

We're not always very generous when we try to explain other people's behavior. It's all too human to think about others in oversimplified and even negative terms. Expending some extra effort thinking about what other things might be going on could help you preserve a relationship.

Your explanations color your opinions of people, and vice versa. If you've concluded that the foreigners you work with rub you the wrong way, that's going to shape the kinds of explanations you come up with for their behavior. And, the more negative explanations you come up with, the less you'll like them.

If you think someone only acts out of self-interest,

chances are, you're going to think less of them. This can influence what you say, what you do and don't do, your body language. All these things can get in your way of developing relationships with people. If you look at their behavior from a different angle, you might discover that they really aren't a "bad person." And whether they are or not, you still have to work with them.

When you come up with overly simple and negative explanations, it's often a clue there are likely other factors at play, and that you could benefit from ruminating on it a little longer. So, if you spot yourself coming up with them, take that as a prompt to set them aside and consider of other reasons. Why else might the person have acted as they did?

"My first thought was that he was trying to skim money," says Army Captain Ryan Casper. Casper was assigned as a mentor to an Afghan company commander. He had been working with the Afghan officer, Wahidi, for several months and the two had developed a friendly relationship with a great deal of mutual respect. The two frequently discussed political matters and often shared stories about their families.

As part of planning and preparing for a field exercise, Casper and Wahidi were discussing the unit's state of supplies. They agreed they needed two or three more sleep tents. Buying the tents would be straightforward, as the unit had Field Ordering Officer (FOO) money to dispose.

"He quickly piped up and said, 'I know where I can get some.'

"I said, 'OK, fantastic,'" Casper remembers.

Casper's job as an advisor was to teach the commander and his unit to be self-sufficient. So, allowing Wahidi to solve this problem on his own seemed appropriate.

Two days later Wahidi came by to show Casper the tents he had bought. Casper was taken aback.

"I wasn't expecting that kind of a tent," he recalls. "They had open ends at the bottom on each end and it gets really cold there at night. So, I asked, him 'You're going to have your men sleep in that?'

"Oh, my soldiers will be fine," Wahidi responded. "That's good quality material." The first thought that flew into Casper's mind was that Wahidi had bought the cheaper tents so he could keep the difference for himself.

After stewing on it a bit, though, this explanation didn't quite sit right with him. The tent incident was the first time since the two had met that he had found himself questioning Wahidi's character. Skimming money. It felt like there had to be something else going on.

Casper put his thinking cap on. In a short period of time he came up with three alternative reasons why Wahidi might have chosen the tents with the open ends. Doing this helped him avoid a knee-jerk reaction that could have soured a good relationship.

"Maybe this is related to machismo," Casper thought to himself. Maybe Wahidi really did think the tents were good enough for the men to sleep in. They could tough it out. "Or, another possibility," Casper says, "maybe his perception of quality was very different than my perception of quality. Maybe he really thought these tents were top-notch." On top of that, Casper also realized that it was possible that Wahidi had bought the tents from a friend whom he was trying to help financially.

Although Casper had a funny feeling, he went ahead and approved the tents. But he vowed to next time have Wahidi get a couple of different cost estimates before making a purchase. Casper continued to have a good relationship with Wahidi and never saw any other evidence of potentially sketchy behavior.

If Casper had stuck with his first explanation—that Wahidi was skimming money for personal gain—he might have reacted very differently. Thinking of other possibilities helped Casper respond more carefully.

When you're unsure about what's going on, or even where to start, take a shotgun approach. Try to think of as many different causes for the same behavior as you possibly can. If you can only think of one single reason for the behavior you saw, take it as a clue. You're more than likely missing something. Any one reason is likely a simplification. There's more going on than meets your eye.

In addition to thinking up several explanations for a behavior, it can also pay off to take the time to figure out how key pieces of a puzzle fit together. How one factor influences another.

Think about it this way. Say you were to explain what propels a car. You could simply say, "The engine." Aside from being a borderline cheeky response, it's not super helpful. Not if you wanted to take some kind of action to change anything about how the car was propelled—say, to increase the car's top speed, or make it operate more efficiently. A useful explanation might sound more like this:

A car is propelled by an engine that uses internal combustion. Inside the engine, small amounts of air and gasoline are injected into tiny, enclosed spaces. After a piston compresses the fuel-air mixture, a spark plug creates a spark that ignites and explodes the gas, causing combustion. The explosion forces the piston back out. The repetition of this cycle again and again creates power that propels the car.

This explanation gives you some hints about parts of the process that you might influence to effect change. Explanations that only capture surface features and gloss over the underlying mechanisms tend to be much less useful for taking action.

As with cars, some explanations of people are more useful than others. They give you more starting points for figuring out what's going on. They focus your attention on the underlying issues, and they give you more options for taking action.

Take a moment to think about the possible underlying causes for behaviors you see. Things a person might have seen, heard, participated in, or have otherwise been exposed to. These experiences can influence their thoughts and emotions, and they can motivate them to behave in certain ways.

Then, think about other factors that might be outside of the person's control. Aspects of their situation, such as their living conditions, their economic status, other people in their environment, or the state of affairs of the society they live in. Sometimes it can pay off to think about what was happening in a region before you arrived. It might help you explain why people do the things they do today.

Master Sergeant Carson enlisted to see the world, and the Army delivered. "After I joined Special Forces, I've been on every continent except for Antarctica," he says. He spent almost all of 2003-2007 in Afghanistan.

"You want to talk about something that's very frustrating? You think you're doing something that would be helpful, and you find out that you've done something that's caused a lot of turmoil. "I built a well in one village, and who would think that that would be a problem?" he asks. Afghan villagers shooting at each other certainly hadn't been part of his plan.

It was four or five months into Carson's second tour. His team was operating in a region that had several small villages in close proximity to each other. One of the villages had been asking for a well for some time. It fit nicely with Carson's orders—install generators and build schools and wells to develop the area. Build the people up so they can sustain themselves and diminish reliance on the Taliban.

Carson and his team had several meetings with the village elders before the well was constructed. "When I look back, I can completely connect the dots, but at the time I did not," he says. "Looking back in hindsight I did notice that they were buying their water, but I didn't know it was from this one specific place."

In the weeks after the well was put in, there was a rise in reports of violent incidents in the villages. It was mostly skirmishes at first.

"Three weeks to a month later I knew for sure there was a problem," Carson says with a hint of regret. "There was a big enough firefight. Two families and several sons ended up shooting at each other. That was the straw that broke the camel's back."

Carson's team forced a meeting with leaders from all the villages. He went into the meeting chalking the activity up to intertribal conflict. Or maybe the Taliban was somehow involved. Even so, Carson knew that it was important to not come across as accusatory in the meeting. He wanted to let the Afghans discuss their problem and listen. He spent hours of listening to the back and forth between the village representatives. Slightly delayed by feverish efforts on the part of the translator to keep up, Carson pieced together the story.

There was another village a few kilometers up the mountainside. They were actually at the head of the river, and that had been their power base. They had used their access to water to trade with villages and communities. When Carson's team put a well in another village, their water was no longer needed. It upset the entire economic trade balance.

"What it really boils down to," Carson reflects, "the village that lost their status was pissed off, and the other villages were pissed off as well because they weren't getting their cut."

In hindsight, the dots connected. Carson realized that the villages each had different strengths, and that's how they got along.

"It kind of kicked us right in the face," he says. "We were just thinking like Americans and thinking that a well would be a good thing. Nobody was prepared for that kind of impact."

His first thought was to take the cursed well out and let things return to the status quo. But that wasn't a viable option.

Instead, they held another meeting a few days later, armed with a deeper understanding of the factors in play. The goal was to negotiate trade back into a state where everyone could feel they benefited.

"They ended up dividing the well," Carson says. "And they all agreed on who was going to cater to who and what the prices were." The elders left the meeting appearing happy about the agreements. There were no more gun fights between them while Carson was there.

"Thinking back, I realize I was locked into a particular linear methodology for fixing things," he says. "This experience really taught me that that's not going to work in every context." He adds, "I'm ticked at myself that I didn't ask more questions."

On subsequent missions Carson did his best to expand his assessments and enrich his models of how things work. "If people wanted schools, or whatever, I wouldn't do anything until I had met with all of the village chiefs so they could discuss what their goals were. So, I could say hey, tell us more about this, what else happened? What else does this connect to?"

This lesson helped Carson in more ways than one. Going forward, he's found that getting a deeper understanding of the dynamics between the leaders in an area also helps him be more targeted and effective with his combat missions.

Sharks hunt at the surface. So, when you dive in shark-infested waters, your strategy for staying safe is simple. You spend minimal time up top and hurry to go deeper.

The same goes when you're trying to figure out what's going on with people around you. Especially ones who might think differently than you do. Staying shallow in your interpretations of their behavior leaves you vulnerable. It leaves you at risk of drawing conclusions that lead you to poor or even disastrous decisions.

Get past your initial interpretations for others' behavior. Push yourself to get to the bottom of things. You know that you've made your way toward a deeper explanation when you've taken several potential causal factors into account. And, you've considered how these possible causes might work together to influence the behavior.

As you think through different causal factors and their effects on one another, you might naturally direct your attention to cultural elements. That is, you might begin to suspect that a person did something because that's what people in that part of the world do. This means you're thinking about them as members of a culture. Being part of a culture means people share certain beliefs and ways of behaving. These may well be different than those you're used to seeing, hearing, and thinking about.

Grab onto the idea that culture might be at play. Seize it. This can be a valuable line of thinking to pursue because it's apt to get you out of the ruts in your usual thought process. Consider how local ideas, beliefs, and values come into play. See where it takes you.

Thinking about the values and ideas that matter to people in a region is likely to get you closer to figuring out what's really going on with them. It can get you closer to explaining their behavior the way they might explain it themselves.

Make it part of your routine to think through the ways culture could be shaping the behavior you're seeing. It will help you better anticipate typical behaviors you see within the same culture. It can also help you spot when people's behavior is off in future interactions.

Special Agent Sean Starnes was on the island of Ishigaki when two US minesweepers were prevented from leaving by a throng of leftist Japanese protestors. The port was run by the mayor, who was a known anti-American leftist. After hours of negotiations the two sides were still deadlocked.

Starnes remembers the sight well. "The protestors would absolutely not allow anyone through. They literally formed a human chain," he says.

The consul general at the time concluded that this was illegal under both international agreements in place and Japanese law. He was going to go through the picket line. Starnes and some other agents came along to protect him— from pushing and shoving, if nothing else.

"When we went out there, it turned into a melee," Starnes says. Starnes was on high alert and was constantly assessing the temperature of the crowd. He realized that the protest had gotten out of hand when he saw a protester behaving in a way that was highly uncommon among Japanese.

"He hit a cop on the head. That is just really something you don't see in Japan," Starnes explains.

The policeman showed the man his badge and the man hit him in the head again. Starnes was astonished. "This is just not done. I mean, that is just very antithetical to Japanese culture," he says with amazement. Starnes goes on to lay out all the factors that came together in his mind to alert him that the protester's behavior was unusual.

"Japanese citizens, by and large, have respect for authority. The crime rates in Japan are way below those in the United States or Great Britain or most of Western Europe, and the reason is people don't care to commit crimes. Being an outlaw in Japan is not nearly as romanticized as it is in the United States, culturally.

"Japanese history, through the millennia, has been very centralized, controlled, and they pride themselves on order and discipline and following the law, following the rule. That goes back to the Tokagawa days, the days of the Shogun and samurai. Orderliness is next to godliness in their world view. Always has been.

"The Japanese are very focused on things that will shame you publicly. It is all about how you look in the public eye. That is where your honor derives from, and you are responsible for that. Unlike Arab culture, where it's an external locus of control in a shame-based society. There, your public image is influenced by events or forces you can't necessarily control. In Japan, it is your responsibility to maintain your face and maintain honor for your family, your work crew, and everything like that."

To Starnes, the protester's behavior flew in the face of what he knew about the culture. The way the cop responded to being hit on the head further challenged his expectations.

"Ordinarily," he explains, "this guy is going to get his head caved in by that cop. They don't kid around with state authority over there, and their culture doesn't provide for that kind of freedom of expression, so to speak.

"And, the cop lost face. Because he has this guy who he announced his lawful authority over, and this guy didn't respect that. Now he is in the position to sort of defend his face, defend his honor, and he didn't do that. He just turned around and helped one of the State Department people get out of the crowd. So, it really puzzled me.

"Japanese cops aren't pushovers," he continues. "They train every day in either judo or kendo. So, they are not averse to getting out and putting a thump on anybody.

Plus, Japanese are not real big on initiative. They do what they are told. Any difficult decision a Japanese person has to make they will push it up the chain of command if at all possible."

The cop's passive demeanor suggested to Starnes that the mayor was calling the shots, and that the chief of police had his hands tied.

"I think that the Mayor of Ishigaki was making the decisions and using the protests. He was very anti-US. And I think it was a political move on his part to allow this protest to get out of hand," he explains.

Understanding how out of the ordinary the whole exchange between the cop and the protester was helped Starnes recognize that the riot was about to escalate. It was clear he needed to get the consul general out, fast.

He also realized that it was no use to continue seeking help from just any local cops. "It was our personal relationship with a particular group within Japanese police who we had worked with before, who were not from that island. They actually did stand up to the protestors, and they didn't mind clashing with these guys, and they punched a hole in the picket line long enough for us to get out. If it had not been for them, we wouldn't have gotten off the port."

Why do people do the things they do? The answers can be frustratingly misty. When you work with people who have a different cultural background, the fog only thickens. It can be even easier to miss what's really going on when people have dramatically different thoughts, values, and perceptions than you do. The possible influences on their decisions can seem impossible to make out, and not just to you. People often don't even know themselves why they do what they do.

When you try to understand people's behavior, your explanations will always be incomplete. But even though there will always be this uncertainty, all is not lost. Some explanations for behavior are more useful than others. They help you know what to expect and how to tell when things are wonky. They give you a clearer view of the levers you have for effecting change. They help you work well with others.

Humans are complex creatures. Avoid casting them as simplistic stick figures. When you're trying to understand a person, force yourself to come up with several possible reasons for their behavior. Then, think some more about the possible influences on them. Try to piece together the ways different factors might work together to affect their actions.

Keep in mind that the way people think and act in your hometown, your unit, and even your country is only a small representation of what's possible. The experiences people in a particular part of the world share can sometimes explain the ways an individual person behaves or reacts.

Draw on your knowledge base. Use the things you know about a person, region, or their culture to get a clearer sense of why they might act as they do.

Key Points

- Come up with several possible reasons for a person's actions

- Go past simple stories and describe deeper causes of behavior

- Consider how the culture and situation affect what people are doing

9

GET INSIDE PEOPLE'S HEADS TO GAIN TRUST, INFLUENCE, AND COOPERATION

"A child in the third grade would be sitting right next to a breaker box and they could literally reach out and electrocute themselves if they touched these two open screws. But everywhere we went, all we kept hearing was, 'That's not a problem, all we want are new windows.'"

Air Force Senior Master Sergeant Shaun Krautkremer spent six months in Kyrgyzstan, working as part of a civil engineering team. The team provided construction assistance to outlying areas and had planned a tour of about thirteen schools.

"Every conversation was an adventure," he says.

From Krautkremer's perspective, it looked like windows were the least of the Kyrgyz schools' infrastructure problems. But each place the team visited they were met with the same puzzling request.

Krautkremer was dumbfounded. "Many of the windows were broken, but not necessarily all spidered and gone.

They were single pane, glazes gone, held-in-by-thumb-tacks kind of thing."

The plumbing and electricity on the other hand—that was a different story.

Krautkremer replays how the typical conversation about plumbing would unfold. "We would ask them, what about your plumbing?

"'Oh, that's not a problem,' they'd say. 'That river right there, we go grab water out of that.'

"'But you have a sink right there,' we'd say.

"'Yeah, that hasn't worked in twenty years.'

"'Why is that not a problem?'

"'I don't know, we have lived without it for twenty years. I haven't had it since I worked here.'"

The plumbing was one thing. When it came to the electricity, though, the problem was not just a question of disrepair. In Krautkremer's assessment, the electrical situation was downright dangerous.

"If you had seen some of this," he says with amazement, "and you don't have to know anything about electrical to know this. I have pictures of some of it, because it was so bad it was comical to look at, and I think they knew it too, though. We would say, let's look at your electrical, and they would look at each other like, 'I don't want to show him what our electrical looks like.'"

Each school Krautkremer's team visited presented a

minor variation on the same solution. "They had taken the breaker boxes off the wall, which, a breaker box is a big thing. It was off the wall and sitting there. The fuses were all burned out and they had used nails to jump across the fuses.

"The wiring had gone bad in the school, so they had taken a hammer and smashed a hole in the side of the wall and run wires out of that and then down, and then drilled holes in the windows to come back in to rerun them.

"Some of the breaker boxes were sitting on the windowsills. So, you'd have a desk and the children sitting right next to them.

"Our question when we saw that was, 'I thought you didn't have a problem with the electrical?'

"And they were like, 'No, it works, see? We have lights,'" he recalls, furrowing his brow.

People who have grown up in different cultures have different vantage points from which they're looking at the world. In other words, their unique background and experiences shape what they see, hear, and perceive. What they want to achieve. What their priorities are. What they consider good and poor solutions, and what they think of as problems in the first place.

"It was about our fifth school, I think, we finally realized we are asking the wrong questions," says Krautkremer.

A pattern had emerged, and Krautkremer thought about

the situation from the Kyrgyz' point of view. "It was a cultural difference," he explains. "Plumbing and electricity. I guess because they had lived without it for so long it wasn't a necessity anymore.

"What they needed was warmth. Kyrgyzstan is a very, very cold country, and single-pane glazed windows with the glazing falling out—it felt like being outside walking next to those windows. So, they were thinking, we need warmth before we need light. Windows are going to make my building warmer and a more conducive environment for teaching.

"When we walked in and said, 'What do you need?' Their first thought was, 'I have needed windows for a long time. If I am going to get one thing out of you, I want windows and I want them now.' That was their immediate need. What we thought was a problem was different than what they thought was a problem," Krautkremer says.

He's still not sure how the locals got the idea that they could only ask for one thing. "So, we had to figure out how to ask people what they needed," he says. "After that fifth school we didn't just ask what was wrong. We said, 'We would like to look at your laundry list. We want to look at your electrical system, your plumbing, we want to look at your heating system.'"

In each place, Krautkremer's team made as many improvements as time and resources allowed, making sure to show the schools' maintenance guys how to take care of things once they were gone.

When you're working with people from other cultures, chances are they think about the world differently than you do. Often, they even have different takes on issues where you might think you're on firm, rock-solid ground. Matters where it's tempting to believe there are surely objective, universally accepted truths about what's real and what's right. Like what it means to be rich or wealthy. It means you have accumulated a lot of expensive things, property, and money, right? Wrong. Not everyone sees it that way.

Army Intelligence Specialist Sergeant Hanes worked with a taxi driver who had four children. All boys. Hanes knew that this taxi driver was a very rich man.

"In Arabic and African culture, the more boys you have, the better off you are. Because you know if you fall sick, your children—your boys—will be able to take care of you," Hanes explains. "So, for him, having four children was more than having a million in the bank. That was his wealth. That was his pride. He was always talking about them."

Just like a coin has more than one side, so does most everything else. Cross-cultural SMEs consistently take the perspective of other people so they can see the other sides, and make use of that full awareness.

When you're working across cultures, considering other people's point of view can help you discover better ways to communicate. It can reveal to you what effective questions or messages might be, and the best way to get them across. Sometimes, it can even spark ideas about creative ways to exchange information that might have never otherwise entered your mind.

Marine Staff Sergeant Ricks lost six guys from his unit in Afghanistan. He and the rest of his team wanted to find the people responsible—fast. But the Afghan informants who might know where they could be found seemed themselves to be lost.

"We put out a map and a piece of imagery, a photo of the terrain. It's like they wouldn't recognize it. It just didn't compute. It was extremely frustrating," Ricks recalls.

In that situation, it might have been tempting to write off the Afghans as useless, to conclude they just weren't bright enough to help. But Ricks instead thought about things from the Afghans' perspective. He considered their background, and how that shaped what they knew and what they didn't.

"I realized," he recalls, "they had never been in the air. They didn't know what their own house looks like from the roof. They could not comprehend an overhead view of a neighborhood."

Taking their perspective helped Ricks diagnose where the kink in the line was. And this helped him come up with a way to get around it.

"We were in a time crunch. So, I paid this guy to rig his camera to his helmet and then drive around and video the entire neighborhood.

"Then we showed it to the sources. If we had information that a person lived in a certain community, then we started the video there.

"We'd ask, 'Do you know where you are?'

"And they'd say, 'Yes, you need to go a half hour that way on motorcycle.'"

In this way, Ricks and his team were able to narrow the field down to a specific set of target locations.

Ricks took the Afghans' perspective, and it helped him understand how they might interpret information put in front of them. This allowed him to come up with a different, more effective way to communicate.

Taking another person's perspective can also help you develop deeper relationships and trust. Once you've tried to figure out where someone might be coming from, you'll be able demonstrate to them that you appreciate their reality. You can show you understand their difficulties and their feelings about the situations they find themselves in. That can make people feel cared about and listened to.

Marine Corps Colonel Louis Boros was helping the Albanian government make their military more up to date and efficient. To do that, many existing systems had to go. When it came time to review the country's air power, Boros faced an emotional former chief of the Albanian Air Force. A general who was watching the world as he knew it crumble around him. Even though Boros wasn't the cause, he was the bearer of the bad news.

"I couldn't solve their problem. From their point of view, somebody's cousin was going to lose his job or was going to lose a position," Boros says regretfully.

The country had gone from a standing army of 180,000 down to just over ten thousand in the last few years. Boros knew this had caused great personal and economic turmoil for people in the military, and most people who have a job in Albania support an extended family. Many people's lives were affected by the downsizing.

When they got to talking about the human cost, the general started tearing up. Boros was unprepared for this, and it momentarily took him aback.

"I did not expect him to get quite that emotional about it. It is incredibly unusual to see an Albanian man getting emotional in that sense. These are macho men, you know," Boros explains.

Boros thought about how he would feel if he was in the general's shoes; if it was his military, his life's work that was being downsized to nothing.

"I think it helped that I was sympathetic to his emotion. He understood that I understood, and I did. I did understand. It has got to be incredibly jarring to work your entire adult life at something that is being done away with and really not even recognized by your own nation as having been important. That has got to be tough. Very tough."

Boros knew that the general had almost six thousand hours under his belt flying MIG-19s. He knew that this was terribly unusual and must be something the general felt proud of. He was very complimentary of the accomplishment.

"I could not offer any solutions for the problem, but I could offer sympathy. I could have been brutal and just said, look, general, your airplanes are junk, they should be in a museum, and all your pilots should be in a museum. Instead, I sympathized and said, yes, I understand you are great pilots."

Boros and the general bonded that day. "Whenever we met after that he made a special point to come over and shake my hand," he recalls. Boros still values this relationship, and it set him up to develop amicable relationships with the general's successors.

Try to figure out what's going on with people. Take their perspective. It can seem like it's a simple lesson. It's true, it's not rocket science. Still, it is something you have to put your mind to and consciously commit to doing. Because it can be easier to skip right past this than you might think.

Once you're in front of something, your own usual way of looking at things will color your perception. Immediately.

Whether it's an abstract idea like your understanding of the importance of windows or the meaning of wealth or a real physical thing like a map. All the signs and cues about what it is and means will point you in a certain direction. Toward a single, unmistakable interpretation. It can be easy to be blinded by the obviousness of it.

When you're working across cultures, resist the impulse to think of your point of view as fact. Be deliberate about looking at things from more than one perspective. Take a measured moment to think about how the people around you might be seeing things. Ask yourself, what could they be thinking? What might be important to them? How are they possibly interpreting this? The answers won't always come easy. Sometimes you may need to think about it for a day or two.

"They were convinced we were going to take advantage of them," Army Major General Ed Dorman remembers. Dorman was leading a project in Afghanistan to convert all the private security companies to a state-run enterprise called the Afghan Public Protection Force (APPF). He quickly discovered that the Afghan companies who would be contracting with the APPF were not keen on the contracting system he had proposed, and he was struggling to understand where they were coming from.

"We had developed a model that said if I am a company that needs some type of security force, I won't hire my own security force, per se," Dorman explains. "What I will do is hire an advisor. He has worked security all his life. He can come in and be a principal advisor on security. Then I will ask him to go to the APPF and deal with the government and draw up the contract."

The Afghan government would not accept that model. Their response was, "We can't let any third parties do the negotiations. We need the principal owner of the company or the company itself to come in and do all the negotiations and draw up the contracts."

"I just couldn't fathom it," Dorman says.

One day he was looking at the PowerPoint presentations his staff had put together to try to explain the concept. "I tried to place myself in their position," he says.

"We put relational diagrams, like a triangle representing the security advisor, and a circle the company, and a square for the APPF or state-owned enterprise. Those three entities, those were all represented as separate and distinct."

When he looked at the diagram from the Afghan ministers' perspective, he suddenly realized that they might be interpreting things differently. That they might see an advisor as not a part of the company. "I think they thought they were a separate entity that could at some point do something they couldn't control," Dorman says.

Once he shifted perspective, Dorman further realized that another element of their plan that could be giving them pause was the way advisors were hired. They would subcontract to the companies. "They didn't want a lot of subcontractors running around out there. They still saw that as an armed militia that was out there to potentially rear its ugly head, I suppose."

So, he and his team went back to the drawing board and made some changes. Instead of outsourcing to subcontractors, security advisors would have to be hired as employees of the companies, and the team removed anything that could look like a subcontractor or a third-party entity from the diagram.

"It eventually turned out OK," says Dorman. "We instituted it, and the ministers got exactly what they wanted."

You have to get inside people's heads to figure out how they interpret things and what they value. As Dorman found, it might be very different from how you see things or what you value. So how do you get inside their heads? A logical place people often start when they try to take someone else's perspective is to ask themselves the question: What would I be thinking if I were them?

Starting with the idea that another person might think and feel and want the same things you do can be an excellent strategy. Often, even if other people look and act very different from you, underneath it all you have a lot in common. Like you, they also feel embarrassed if they're called out on mistakes. Like you, they also want to keep their families safe.

Once you've taken an initial step in their shoes, keep it going. To get closer to what they might be thinking, you have to get out of your own head, so to speak, and inside theirs. Luckily, you don't have to be a shrink to do that.

To start, find out more about them. If you have a certain person or people you're working with, you can dig into their specific background. Talk to people who've worked with them before—to people who know them. You might be able to learn about where and how they grew up, where they went to school (if they did), if they are married, if they have kids.

Knowing a bit about someone's background can give you some general ideas about their preferences and ways of thinking about things. Your interpretations of how these factors influence their point of view will still be based on your own framework for thinking. To really get behind their eyes, you'll need to account for culture.

Cultural knowledge can help you better understand someone's perspective. You might have some general information you've read or heard in a class about the region. You might also have gathered some knowledge about the culture and region from experience, from being there. You can learn all kinds of things about people by keeping your eyes open.

Factoring in clues you have about a person's culture can help you start accounting for possible differences between your perspective and theirs. You can use cultural information to track down the alternative direction the other person's thoughts may have taken and adjust the first guess you came up with.

Imagine that you've just started an assignment in Burkina Faso. You have many tasks. One of them is to dispense microloans to stimulate small business growth. You know that in some way the loans are really start-up donations in disguise. A secondary goal of the program is to educate the locals about effective business practices.

Oumar is a local entrepreneur who is having trouble getting his carpentry business off the ground.

"My organization will be happy to give you a loan," you tell Oumar. "It will help you cover your initial expenses."

Your translator passes the message in Jula, the local language. Oumar instantly shakes his head and looks worried.

You turn to your translator. "Does he know what a loan is?" you ask.

"Sure," he replies, "we know about loans here." He proceeds to tell you the word for loan in Jula.

"Well. What does that mean?" you probe.

Your translator explains that the Jula word for loan means a cord that's attached between two people. When a person accepts a loan from another, there now exists a bond, a cord between them. In order to sever that cord the person must focus all their attention on repaying it in some capacity.

If Oumar accepts your loan, he will be thinking about you, personally, every day until it's paid off.

Ooph. Something has clearly got lost in translation. When was the last time you even thought about your personal relationship with your creditors?

Lieutenant Colonel Rudy Atallah had the experience of learning the true meaning of loans when he was working in West Africa. When he did, he changed his approach.

As he explains, "In learning the language, I learned the culture, and learning the culture, I learned to associate with them differently. So, if I gave them something, I always processed that this was not a loan, this was a gift. This is from me to you. This is part of me to you and that was always an amicable exchange that opened up greater dialogue."

Each of us experiences the world around us in our own unique way. But we all grow up to see the world through glasses that are tinted a certain way by where we come from. This means there are patterns in the ways people from certain regions and cultures see things.

Learn a bit about the culture and try to take the unique circumstances people contend with into account. This can help you get a better sense of what it might be like to truly take a walk in their shoes.

Early in Lieutenant Colonel Page's career he had an experience in Southeast Asia. It was a small, seemingly insignificant encounter that turned into a mind-altering moment. One that profoundly influenced his appreciation for what it might be like to walk a different path in life.

"One of my friends had been stationed in the Philippines, and I would go down to visit him. We were walking out through this extremely poor Filipino area outside the naval base one day, and we were just talking about the nature of the poverty in the Philippines, and the lack of justice, etc.

"And my friend said, 'If you and I had the level of education that we have, you know, college education and experience, and we were Filipino and lived here? We would probably belong to the rebel group, too.'"

The friend's observation struck a chord with Page. "I remember that conversation explicitly. It is all about your perspective and where you came from. I guess that helped me to be able to sideline my preconceived American notions of what is right and wrong, and how things should work."

This exchange helped Page gain deeper appreciation for the complexity of people's motivations. He credits it with paving the way for him to make more accurate assessments and have smoother interactions with people in disparate places in the world. In his estimation, the tough interactions he had were with people who didn't try to take others' perspectives.

He recalls of his time working in Djibouti, "I had more of a difficult challenge dealing with Americans during that period than I did with the Africans. Especially Americans in the intelligence community back in the States, who were telling me who were the good guys and who were the bad guys.

"Their thinking process was that anybody who had ever done any business with—and I will use the generic term al-Qaeda—must be a terrorist themselves, or support terrorism, and therefore deserves our attention, if not our wrath.

"For example, if they could associate a ship with moving weapons for al-Qaeda, even one time, then they must be doing this all the time. Therefore, the head of that shipping company must be an al-Qaeda supporter, and we need to build a target package on that guy.

"In reality, that was so far from the truth. The guy that owned the shipping company was just a businessman. Things are not as clear cut in the third world. You make a living, and sometimes that means you do things for shady people, and vice versa, and that doesn't necessarily make you a supporter of terrorism around the world.

"You have to constantly be putting yourself in their shoes. You have to say, if I lived in this world at this time, in their world, what would I do? How would I act? Where would my loyalties be?"

Figuring out what goes on in other people's heads can be a challenging puzzle. You'll probably never become a mind reader. The chances are slim that you'll know exactly what another person is thinking in a given moment. But you can get closer—much closer than if you didn't give the other person's perspective a second thought.

Putting yourself in another person's shoes helps you streamline your communications with them. It can also help you cement relationships, gain trust, and persuade people to cooperate with your plans.

Don't you feel better throwing in with people who at least make an attempt to understand your background, beliefs, and values?

Make perspective-taking part of your routine. When you're engaging across cultures, take a breather now and then. Try to see things from their point of view.

Ask yourself, "What would I be thinking right now?" Then ask, "What if I were really in their shoes, all the way?"

Key Points

- A person's background shapes how they view the world

- Take another's perspective by thinking about what they know, want, and feel

- Use what you know about a person's culture to put yourself all the way in their shoes

10

WHY YOU SHOULD ENGAGE OTHERS BEFORE YOU KNOW ENOUGH

Imagine a father teaching his son how to ride a bike. The father is thorough in everything he does. So, he starts by educating the boy on the physics of how a bicycle remains upright.

He patiently and as simply as possible explains gyroscopic theory. He shows pictures and short movie clips to illustrate the principle. Using his own bike, he demonstrates how a riderless bicycle balances itself, steers automatically and corrects itself for wobbles, until it loses speed and eventually falls flat on its side.

When he finally pulls out the red Lightning McQueen bike with built-in racing sounds that he's been hiding in the garage, his son's reaction leaves him speechless. The boy reports that he's not sure he'll be very good at riding a bike. It seems pretty hard. He's not sure he knows how it works well enough.

Paralysis by analysis. It can happen to all of us in many

different types of situations. When you're working in a new culture, the complexity of people's behavior and the strange ways things seem to work can be overwhelming. The counter-intuitive thing is—when you pick up a little bit of knowledge, it can occasionally crush your confidence.

Say you do a little bit of homework on your own about a new place you'll be working. Or, maybe you get an introduction, like a predeployment brief or an in-country familiarization course. These study activities might highlight to you how different this new place and its people are from what you're used to. This can lead you to focus on how much you don't yet know or understand, and that can pull you to a standstill.

Go in with your eyes wide open to this potential side effect of arming yourself with information. Whether you face getting on a bicycle, or you're let loose in Japan for the first time, try not to focus on the unknowns. Push yourself to engage with the culture even if you feel that you haven't completely mastered it. Even when you feel like you're out of your depth.

Senior Chief Petty Officer Vincent is a personnel specialist in the Navy. The first time he was assigned in Japan, he got an orientation soon after he walked off his ship in Yokosuka.

"We got this in-country-brief when we got there," he says. "It's required for everybody that is PCSing. It's a week's worth of class and they kind of give you some phrases. What's the bathtub called, what is a Japanese house, and all that.

"If you have your family with you, you get all this cultural stuff sort of thrown in. Because it is totally different there, where they drive, how to rent out in town, what are your obligations, what are your requirements? The parking issues. All these things are part of that culturalization that you are bombarded with in that one week."

Going through the class that first time around, Vincent felt like he only learned just enough Japanese to shop. "I learned *hi, hello, good morning*, all that. I would say the niceties. Like, 'excuse me' is *sumi masen*. Asking where, how, how much, and all that. I learned the phrase 'I don't speak Japanese.' Those things."

The words and phrases he picked up seemed woefully inadequate when he faced the perplexing Japanese train system for the first time. He had arranged to meet an acquaintance outside a local zoo in Yokohama and wanted to use the local transportation to get there.

Walking into the terminal, he was immediately overcome. Throngs of people flowed past him, in and out, up and down escalators. Fast. Colorful arrows accompanied by inscrutable Japanese characters pointed in all directions.

He quickly realized that he needed some help. So, he started approaching some of the locals using the tidbits of information and language he'd picked up in class.

"I used what I learned. 'Excuse me, sumi masen.' Then I showed them like a map that I was holding. I bowed first, that is the tradition, and said sumi masen, where is, *doko*, zoo? Then at the end say please, *onegai shimasu*. So—sort of that way—I need help to find the zoo, can you help me please?"

He soon found that his attempts were met with a less-than-warm reception.

"They would start shaking their head, give me a sign, no, no, no, and walk away from me," he recalls. Vincent quickly formed a theory about what could be going on.

"I was trying to speak some Japanese. I wasn't fluent, but trying. There is a big difference," he laughs. "And my interpretation was, because they can't respond in English, they responded in Japanese, and they anticipated that I may not be able to understand. So, my take on that is they didn't want to engage in English in a conversation with a foreigner because they don't speak the language. Or they may understand but didn't want to speak it."

So, Vincent changed his tack. He looked around and eyed a group of Japanese teenagers.

"I approached them, and they were like, oh yeah! Some of them were like, rowdy, and I just repeated my phrases and pointed, and in broken English they told me what I needed to do."

Vincent didn't give up, and it paid off. He felt this

experience gave him the confidence to take the train more often. That, in turn, gave him more freedom, and a better experience on his assignment overall.

"It helped, and it reduced my fear quite a bit of exploring or going around. Because at that point, there were two options to get to the other base. I could take the shuttle, or I could ride the train. This experience kind of gave me the confidence to—OK, let's go for the train. It gave me the freedom to say, I don't have to wait for the bus. Heck no. So, it made me braver. More confident."

His confidence and practice using the train system immersed him further into the culture. It also came in handy for professional reasons one day when he had to get from Yokohama down to Yokosuka in a hurry.

"I needed to get down to the base in Yokosuka to pick up tickets for our guys that were flying out the following day when their ship pulled in. I needed to be there before the office closed, so I'd be able to hand out their tickets right there, as they were leaving the ship. Or else they were going to miss the bus to go to Tokyo."

Vincent couldn't use the shuttlebus, because it didn't run on weekends. But luckily, he'd built up his confidence to become a regular user of the local train service.

"So, I hopped on the train all the way down to Yokosuka and made it to the office. I think I had maybe half an hour before they closed."

Moving forward when it seems like you're on shaky ground can feel awkward. Embarrassing even. On the whole, what's most at risk is your pride.

As Navy Captain Pete Miller puts it, "You have to be willing to put yourself out there and take a chance. Sometimes you will make mistakes, but if you are vulnerable and have some humility in the recovery—your ego can recover."

The rewards are difficult to quantify. But time and again, you'll find that moving outside of your comfort zone can help you make significant progress on your relationships and your agenda.

Navy Petty Officer First Class Akiyama's local partners had invited him and his shipmates out to enjoy a local meal in Indonesia. As they all got seated around the table, Akiyama noticed that the restaurant had set out forks and spoons next to the colorful napkins and dinnerware in anticipation of their Western guests. The group was eagerly anticipating the spread they were about to experience. Everything appeared normal. Until the servers brought out a set of peculiar water bowls.

"This gentleman came out with a bowl. Kind of a small, like, glass bowl, I'd say, and it had a lime floating in like a water solution. So, he set it on the table, and we were all like, what is that for?

"I was like, it can't be a drink. I didn't know if it was like a course in the meal we were having, or oh, it's going to be a refreshing drink or something," says Akiyama.

Puzzled, he enquired. "I asked the company that we were with, what's that?

"And they said, 'Oh, it's for washing your fingers.'

"I go, 'Why do I need to wash my fingers?'

"They said, 'Oh, actually we don't use utensils here in this country, we eat with our hands.'

"Oh, really, OK.

"And they said, 'Well, you want to try?'"

Akiyama had traveled all over Asia and Africa working in the supply corps—food service logistics, specifically. He had seen and participated in eating with his hands in other countries. He wasn't sure how it was done in Indonesia, but he was up for the challenge. His shipmates' eyes got really big as they processed what happened next.

"So, I said, 'Yeah, I guess,' and then suddenly all the utensils and cutlery were removed from the table and we had the opportunity to learn how to eat with our fingers. So that was a noble experience there."

They all then got a lesson in the custom around eating with your hands in Indonesia. "There is a particular way to kind of scoop and mash rice and kind of almost flick into your mouth to get it off your fingers.

"It's kind of your three fingers, index middle, and then your ring finger goes through the three or four working parts along with the thumb, so you take those three fingers and the thumb, and you almost form a triangle or square in a mashing motion, is where you kind of grip the rice and then whatever sauce or meat is going in and it all goes in, in one shot."

Akiyama was fascinated, and his shipmates eventually took to it.

"They were initially kind of like, oh, what's going on," he remembers. "You know. it's like anytime you see somebody do something they are not used to it. They kind of fumbled, and did a little giggle here and there, that kind of thing."

But they did it, and Akiyama was pleased. "You know when you're in the presence of somebody from another country, another culture, you act a bit different than you might when you're with a friend or family. Why be rude, you know?"

Akiyama didn't know exactly how you eat with your hands in Indonesia. But he was pretty sure he could carry it out based on his past experiences. His shipmates were uncertain. They were challenged, but they persevered. In the end they all made a favorable impression on their partners, and they picked up a new skill.

Participate when you can, and don't worry about your pronunciation, your skills, or how much you know about the activity in question. Let people show you. Let them teach you. It's sure to expand your connections and your horizon, and it might help you move beyond the pier.

"When we travel to foreign ports, it's common for people to go on the pier," Marine Corps Major General Bell explains. "They buy souvenirs, make a phone call, or check the internet. Maybe they experience the night life. For many, that's enough.

"Some want to go farther—get away from the pier and go inland. The people I like working with do this. They are more curious. They recognize there are differences, including the logic of the people and language, and want to better understand those differences. They want to find out why the people are the way they are. What is the society like? What are they motivated by?"

"When you're getting up to speed in a new culture, you really have to be fearless, and just do it," Bell says. "Don't worry at all if it's not perfect or even good." He notes that simply attempting to address a cultural norm or to speak a little of the language is generally appreciated. Even if you aren't quite getting it right.

Bell has seen this firsthand more than once. For example, when he was assigned in Norway for eighteen months, he had made it a habit to use a local greeting whenever he started meetings with his foreign partners.

"It was the custom there," he explains, "to greet with 'Good morning, gentlemen.' In Norwegian, of course."

So that's what he did. For many months.

"On my last day one of the foreign officers came up to me and asked me if I wasn't going to bid my rabbits good morning today."

Bell sensed that a smirk lurked underneath the man's stone-faced expression.

"I said, 'What do you mean?'

"And he said, every day you come in here and instead of 'gentlemen,' which would be *herrar*, you say *harer*.'" Bell pronounces each perfectly and distinctly. It's clear that he now knows the difference.

"Instead of *gentlemen* I was saying *rabbits*. It's almost the same word, but it has a different meaning," Bell explains and laughs. He feels confident that his Norwegian colleagues appreciated his attempt, even though it was flawed and cause for chuckles. They felt comfortable enough to inform him of his blunder.

You've picked up some words and phrases. You've learned some bits and pieces about the national holidays. The local history. The customs. Use them. Weave them into conversation and ask questions about them.

Try to shake hands the way they do it. Attempt to position your legs properly when you sit down. Your efforts are appreciated. They show you cared enough to know a little. Even if your execution is off, you're highly likely to earn some points, because it shows you're interested.

Air Force Master Sergeant Shaun Krautkremer knows

that attempts go a long way. "I have been to so many countries, so many places, and I think that has really helped me," he reflects.

"Realizing that I am in your neighborhood, so I am going to do things the way you do it. To the best of my ability. Even though you feel like you look foolish, in their eyes, you try to do it that way. Even if you do it wrong, you are trying."

Navy Captain Dan Braswell has drawn a similar life lesson from his many years working abroad. "Try to get it right, but don't let perfection be the enemy of the good. That was my approach. I always tried to get it right, and if I was talking to somebody, I'd ask them, 'Am I getting this right?' Just to show them that I was interested."

By trying out some of the new things you've learned, even if it feels uncomfortable, you demonstrate that you are aware of people's culture. This shows that you're trying to relate, and that can open doors in ways you might not expect.

As Army Lieutenant Colonel Jim Dunn puts it, "You don't have to be an expert." That's a beautiful feature of this strategy. All you have to do, he says, is "know enough to make an inference or to make a comparison of 'Oh, gee, this reminds me of,' or 'Isn't this kind of like that?' Even if you are wrong, the people that you are talking to, the impression they gain of you is, 'OK, this is someone who knows what is going on, and who is interested.'"

The cross-cultural SMEs agree that putting yourself out there and using your cultural knowledge, even when it's limited, can pay off big time. But, when you do put yourself out there, sometimes you're going to stick your foot in it. It's inevitable. Luckily, the consequences of slip-ups are mostly in your head.

Say you accidentally use an impolite hand gesture. You mispronounce a word and unintentionally make an ill-placed or even obscene remark. Your attempt to get yourself seated in the cross-legged position is less than graceful and you allow the local village leaders to catch a glimpse of the soles of your feet. Will the whole world come crashing down on you? Doubtful.

Sometimes it's tempting to focus on how much you don't know and can't do, and to imagine that the consequences of making a mistake are way more serious than they really are. This can paralyze you. Don't let it. A lot of the time, when you get things wrong, the worst thing that happens is that people chuckle.

This has been Navy Master Chief Petty Officer Dale Carter's experience. "People always appreciate somebody that tries," he says. "Even though it's just like myself. I'm very lousy at language skills. They appreciate it and found it very humorous most of the time, and that's one way of opening the door, honestly."

And this presents an opportunity. It means that you have more control over the fallout of mistakes than you might think. In fact, getting things wrong can be the foundation for great relationships. If you play things right. Like Army Lieutenant Colonel Ike Merrill.

"I murdered Dari like you wouldn't believe," he chuckles. "And every time the translators and everybody would sit down and say, 'Well, you've got to say it this way because if you don't, you're saying this instead,' and then they just laugh. Because you say silly things, you know."

OK, alright, so people laughed at him. What's Merrill's secret sauce here? Well, it's what he did in response that's the key. "Of course, you laugh with them. The next thing you know, you are great friends," he explains.

When you laugh at yourself people get more comfortable around you. This makes it more likely they will tell you that you're wrong. Correct you. Show you how it's really done. And that means now you're learning something. Double whammy. They're more comfortable and you're learning something.

Be prepared to use the information you've picked up, however insignificant it may seem. On the flip side, be honest with yourself and others. When you don't know something, you don't know. Admit it when there's a gap in your cultural understanding. It's OK. Being honest about the limits of your knowledge can also pull people in.

Navy SEAL Commander Russell had connected with one of the many princes in Qatar. The two had an initial conversation where the prince talked eagerly and in great detail about his deep passion: falcons. Russell expressed polite curiosity.

"I knew nothing about falconeering," says Russell. Hunting with falcons sounded cool, but it wasn't something Russell had ever thought about. He knew nothing about it. But he knew that people like to talk about themselves.

"You can express your genuine lack of knowledge and let them tell you more about it," Russell explains.

Four days later the prince's aide called him up. Russell was invited to join an excursion into the Qatari desert so the prince could show him his proud possessions. Russell admitted to the prince that he didn't know much about falcons. As it happened, the prince was more than happy to teach him. The result? They developed rapport.

When you're faced with complexity in a new culture, keep an eye on the tiny things you do know. Think of them as starting points. The little information you have can help you get off the ground and give you momentum. Maybe you know a phrase or two you can use to start a conversation. Or maybe you've learned some facts you can use as a basis for asking questions and picking up new bits of understanding. It might even be something as simple as a local greeting.

Army Lieutenant Colonel Dunn describes it this way, "Even just greeting someone with *as-salaam alaykum* and responding with the correct thing when they said it. It brought people in my direction. I think they saw it as I was showing them that I knew a little bit about their culture. That I respected it."

In Dunn's experience, the reason people respond positively is that "Nobody likes to work with ignorant people. And the ugly American myth, if it is a myth, is a pretty strong one. Anything that you can do to break that down just makes it easier for you, and that makes it easier for your country." Dunn made headway on building rapport using a local everyday greeting.

Colonel Alex Portelli and Sergeant Tom Audetat have spent their long careers with the Army in disparate places in the world. Portelli served the bulk of his thirty-plus years as a foreign area officer in Europe. Audetat spent many years as an intelligence specialist in the Middle East. In these disparate places and roles, they each found ways to use scraps of information to add a dash of spice to the salutations they used to make connections with people.

Ahead of an assignment in Denmark, Portelli had come across an irresistible tidbit of information. He heard that there was a special greeting that Prince Carl used to address the Norwegians, which translates to *dear compatriot*. Prince Carl was from Denmark and, by appointment of the

Norwegian government, became King Haakon VII of Norway.

Portelli learned that this historical moment is a point of pride for the Danes. So, he boldly used this greeting in meetings with them.

"Every time I got a Dane that came to my international fellows' program, or a met a Dane when we were working together in a group, the first thing that I always said was *kære landsmann*. I got a laugh and a chuckle out of that," he says.

"Everywhere I go I look for the cultural hook. The thing that would show any foreigner that I am dealing with that I'm not the typical American," he says.

Army Sergeant Tom Audetat used a similar strategy in the Middle East to great effect. He also pushed himself to use a special greeting he had picked up from talking to his translators.

"In Iraq," he says, "there is something completely unique. They say, 'How is your color?' And it's completely Iraqi, and so if you learn that, it gleans a little bit of respect. Because you have done at least that little piece of homework, you know? A good greeting, if you learn to say it properly, is a great icebreaker."

Most likely, when you head overseas for your job, you won't have time to become an expert on the local culture, history, or language. Don't let that hold you back. Make it a habit to use the bits you do know. Weave them into your routine. Use them in conversation.

It might seem awkward to throw simple scraps of information and foreign phrases out there. Especially if it feels like you only know the bare-bones basics. But doing so really can move the needle in your favor.

Even if your pockets of knowledge about the culture seem insignificant or random, don't write them off. Even the most left-field insights can sometimes be used as a seed to start a conversation, to find common ground and develop rapport.

Air Force Captain Singer wasn't a huge soccer fan. But when he worked as an intelligence officer in Turkey, he started following it because it was popular. He really didn't know very much about it. He did pick up one important thing from listening to the conversations around him. He learned that the number two soccer team, Trabzonspor, was the favorite in the region of Turkey he was in.

"When I was out and about talking to people, one of the subjects that would come up is soccer, and people would ask me, 'Who do you like?' And I would just say, 'Yeah, Trabzonspor.' Which wasn't a lie. I wasn't a huge football fan, but I started following Turkish football while I was there, and I was, 'Yeah, I root for Trabzonspor.'

"And that, in addition to very elementary Turkish, these guys, their faces lit up and they were just kind of like, take me under their wing and be like, wow, you are one of us now. And I would think to myself, wow, really? That's all it takes, is being polite in their language and maybe liking the same soccer team? And now I am like one of them and getting invited to their house for dinner and tea and stuff like that."

It can sometimes seem like there's a mountain between you and doing the right thing. Saying the things that'll get people to like you, trust you, and respect you feels insurmountable.

If only you knew all the things you don't know. With perfect knowledge you'd get it right every time. You'd be able to fire off that zinger and wow everybody with your brilliance. Unfortunately, perfect knowledge is a pipe dream.

You'll never understand another culture as well as someone who has grown up in it, as someone who's lived it from childhood. And chances are, with all the other things you have to keep on top of, you might not even get close.

Fortunately, reaching out and connecting with foreigners doesn't require you to know their culture inside out. Rapport is something that is created and cultivated over time, and there are many things you can do to stir up some mutually good feelings. Even if you're only slightly familiar with the other person's culture.

Don't be overly critical of what little you know about other people and other cultures. You might overlook simple nuggets you have that can help you build a solid connection. You know a fact, a word, a phrase? Use it. Don't set the bar too high. Try to say something in their language. Make a reference to something they might care about and set aside your fear of goofing up.

That doesn't mean you should pretend to know more than you do. Admit to yourself and others when you don't know something. Then maybe you have a chance to find out. Ask people about their culture. Many will enjoy talking about themselves and their ways.

Take a risk. Get it wrong. Shrug it off and learn from it. Confront your ignorance head on to defeat it. Be ready to be laughed at, and to laugh at yourself. The point is not to show off how much you know or how awesome you are. It's to make a connection, and mutual amusement is a fantastic tool to do that.

Key Points

- Push yourself to engage with the culture even if you haven't mastered it (you never really will)

- People will generally appreciate when you try to work with their customs and language, even if you aren't quite getting it right

- Use what nuggets of knowledge you have about the culture in your dealings and decisions

11

READY, AIM, TALK

Staff Sergeant Dixon wiped his brow. Cambodia was hot. He'd just finished briefing a construction task, when his driver pulled him aside and shared some disturbing news.

"He said to me, 'The captain didn't pass on your message. He actually told the guys that he doesn't want to do it your way,'" Dixon recalls.

"We were building a school from the ground up. It was a one-for-one match with our engineers and their engineers from the Royal Cambodian Army," says Dixon. It was a three-month project, and it was about 70 percent complete.

A Cambodian captain who spoke very good English had sometimes stepped in to translate, passing on Dixon's instructions to the Cambodian crew. Or so Dixon thought. Dixon's immediate reaction was one of anger and frustration.

"I felt kind of like I got stabbed in the back. We were working toward a common goal and somebody basically just told me that my opinion was null and void," Dixon says of the driver's revelation.

Dixon was mad, and he wanted to respond right away. Instead he decided to give it a few hours.

"I wanted to keep a level head. I didn't want to act on my gut," he says. "You know, like a knee-jerk reaction." Though it might have felt good in the moment, yelling wasn't going to solve his problem.

Dixon stepped back and thought through what he really wanted to accomplish. First, he needed to make sure that there weren't two different standards on the construction site.

That helped him clarify who he needed to talk to. He also considered the best way to broach the issue. That captain was just an intermediary. So, Dixon found the engineer who was overseeing the Cambodian carpenters. Instead of pushing demands, he got the engineer talking first.

"I wanted to understand their methods and why they were passionate that it had to be done a different way than I was proposing," Dixon explains.

The task at hand was the creation and installation of a large concrete ceiling beam. Dixon listened to the engineer describe their usual approach.

"The biggest difference in our methods was that we wanted to build a wooden structure on the ground to prefabricate it ahead of time. This would mean less work and less people up on the scaffolding that was three levels high," Dixon explains.

"They wanted to do all the work overhead by using scaffolding."

In the past weeks Dixon had picked up on many differences in how the Cambodians did construction. He had noticed that wearing safety gear like protective eyeglasses, gloves, and hardhats seemed foreign to them. They also didn't tie scaffolding down. They just put it together, raised it and climbed on up.

Dixon continues, "I've done enough work on job sites outside the Army to know there is the right way of doing something and then there is the quick way of doing it. So, I understood where he was coming from, because sometimes the safety precautions are overkill. On the other hand, there's no reason to put people at risk when you don't have to."

"Their engineer understood why the safety was there. But to him it seemed you can save a lot of time by moving forward without these things," Dixon says. He found that the engineer had a lot of technical expertise and the two quickly worked out a compromise solution.

Beyond the immediate issue, Dixon needed to fix the teamwork. How were the two groups going to work together on the project? To get there, he had to close the loop with the captain.

Dixon chose to cast the issue as a possible case of misunderstanding. Perhaps he didn't quite understand what the captain had communicated to his people. Or maybe the captain hadn't quite caught what Dixon's instruction was. Dixon pressed on to suggest that he could use the on-site interpreters to coordinate more with the Cambodian engineer. "I said I thought we could get down to the meat and potatoes a little better considering we were in the same position."

The captain took note and backed off. "He said, 'Well, I'm here to help, let me know if you need anything,'" Dixon says.

Dixon went on to develop a close working relationship with the engineer.

"I couldn't speak construction in Khmer and he couldn't speak construction in English. We just had a very good appreciation of each other's work ethic and valued each other's opinions. It ended up working out. A bond was created, and the mission was accomplished," Dixon concludes.

Dixon first worked out what he wanted to accomplish. He set goals. Then, he determined whom he needed to talk to, and how he was going to approach those conversations. He found it was more than worth it to plan and prepare before firing off a round of words.

Communication is complicated. Even when the situation isn't boiling over. Yet you can nail your objectives by considering how to best express yourself. There are many dimensions to consider. Words or pictures. Dress and style. Body language and gestures. Or even who's in the room. You can look at these as hooks to get your message across. It does take a little thought up front.

Sergeant First Class Wilkins had to stretch beyond words when he worked a short-term construction project in the Philippines. He was working side by side with Filipino soldiers. Collaboration was an important part of the objective. Developing partnerships. He also had to communicate with the local vendors. But communicating about technical aspects of construction was challenging. He did not speak Tagalog, by any stretch, and his interpreter wasn't up on construction lingo.

"Sometimes I'd say, 'I need a piece of pipe,' and the storekeeper would bring me one and I'm like, 'Yes, that is a pipe. But it's not exactly what I meant.'" Wilkins stepped back and thought about what to do. He had to figure out a good way to break it down, so it was more understandable. To figure out what they had or express to them what he was looking for.

"Barney style," Wilkins says, and explains. "I've got kids, and you know, you watch Barney. They break it down to the simplest terms. I'd try to figure the simplest way to explain it." It took a new level of forethought to communicate clearly. If Wilkins needed a pipe fitting, he might ask them for a pipe. Then they'd bring the pipe.

Then he'd point to the end of it. Connector. You connect the two pieces.

"Sometimes they'd have no idea what I was talking about because they didn't use them or use different stuff," Wilkins says. He'd go back to the Filipino Army guys. "They'd be like, yeah, well, we do this, and I'd have them show it to me or draw it up and I'd say, 'OK, that makes more sense.' This is what I should be asking for and it would make more sense to the vendors."

Wilkins first thought carefully about what he was trying to say. Then, he figured out simple ways to explain himself.

When Senior Master Sergeant Arkinson, an Air Force intelligence specialist, arrived in Iraq, he found he was walking into a sour assignment. Not only had his predecessors failed to meet their objectives in working with a local informant, but they had caused the guy to clam up, completely.

Before diving in, he thought a bit about his immediate aims. "The first thing I wanted to do was to show that I was somebody different," Arkinson says. Then he pondered how to do it. The trending facial hair fashions gave him an idea. Beards were all the rage among US servicemembers.

"Everybody going to Iraq, they wanted to beard up. Look local," he recalls, and continues. "It was funny. It's Iraq. We aren't talking about the hills of Afghanistan, where dudes are bearded out as a sign of manhood. Most Iraqis wear a mustache."

With everybody being bearded up, Arkinson chose to go in clean-shaven. "At the time, I was twenty-nine, maybe. So, I didn't have such a young naïve face. I didn't need to use the beard to make myself look older. From a credibility aspect," he explains.

By going in without a beard, he could look like someone who had just flown in. A clean slate. A fresh start. Someone who was going to be different than the guys before him.

Arkinson often had to consider multiple facets of communications. At one point, he was getting ready for an interview with a guy who was accused of doing some pretty dastardly deeds.

"In our eyes, he was a bad guy," Arkinson says, and walks through his assessment. "But he was also a victim of policy. Because of the circumstances in the country, he was forced to take a certain path to do the right thing for his family.

"When you have people come into your house and threaten to kill your entire family, you are going to do what it takes. Even if it results in x, y and z. You all of the sudden become that person you don't want to be."

Arkinson quickly got the feeling that the man wanted to tell the truth. Doing so would help him take a seat farther back on the bad guy bus. But Arkinson had to remove some obstacles. He realized his female interpreter might be problematic. He decided to look for a male replacement.

"How to get them to tell you the truth without feeling shamed? Keeping the cultural things in mind, that is a challenge," he says.

Arkinson knew that the man had a very large family. He had a wife, daughters. He had a mom and sisters. So, in Arkinson's mind having a female in the room would be too emotional.

"He may feel like having the woman there reminds him of his mom," he explains. "I wanted to avoid the emotional connection that would make him less likely to admit it." Considering the effects of the social context, Arkinson planned accordingly. He shaped the circumstances by getting the right person in the room.

Crafting your communication and its optimal delivery can be difficult, especially when you realize that maybe you yourself aren't the best messenger. At times, maybe someone else can better grease the skids. For example, Colonel David Bunn understands the limits of his own ability to fake interest in things he could care less about.

"If I do a host-nation engagement and the guy says, 'Oh man, I think NASCAR is the greatest thing in the world.' Guess who is going to be talking to him? My lance corporal who loves NASCAR. That doesn't mean I sell the responsibility. The corporal still understands, 'Hey, you're going to have to talk to my boss on these issues.'"

When you work with people from other cultures it can

seem like the principles for how to get things done are completely blown out of the water. How do you get on the same page and move forward?

It takes a dash of advanced planning and tweaking your thinking about how you get from A to B a few degrees. Before you open your mouth, locate the lever that's going to get you the effect you're looking for.

Take a moment to think about your objectives. What is it that you're trying to achieve? Then, think about what you know about the person or people you're dealing with. Where they come from. What they're used to, and not used to. Do your best to take their perspective. What could their current thinking on the issue or topic be?

Finally, you're ready to use your cultural knowledge to tune your transmission to the people or person in front of you.

Navy Captain Pete Miller's career as a submarine commander has taken him to corners of the world many people have never even heard of. Like, Monroeville, Liberia, Bizerte in Tunisia, and Dakar, Senegal. Given that backdrop, his first answer when asked about his biggest challenge working across cultures is surprising.

"Australia. It might sound silly, but that really was a different language there and a totally different culture," Miller reflects. Earlier in his career Miller spent two years as an exchange officer in the Royal Australian Navy, stationed in Perth. Some of the guys that had been in that position before him hadn't developed what you would call smooth working relationships with the locals.

"In part, it may be because they kind of had scorn for their diesel submarines," Miller speculates. The director for Pacific Fleet Training at the time was eager for a change in the relationship. "He wanted us to start doing submarine officer training together. Not just 'at' each other, not just pinging on each other, but a real exchange of officer candidates," says Miller.

The director relied on Miller to make this happen. "His guidance to me was," he chuckles, "Go down there, and if you're stumbling around, but making things better and closer, you are not doing anything wrong."

Miller ran into a brick wall right away, the first week he got there.

"I was always getting asked by their submarine force, the locals, and later on, the press, 'Whose submarines are better?' And this really encapsulates the whole issue. Because it was framed in way where they wanted a yes or no answer. They wanted a zero or a one answer, and no matter what you answered, you were wrong," he explains.

"If you are American, you kind of think you own the world, and, you think your submarines are the best," he says.

"You have to understand that Australians are very

proud. Australian culture is sort of, 'We are going to go it alone.' And in Perth, in Western Australia, even more so, right? It's five hours by plane from Sydney." Miller lets the implication hang in the air.

"I figured out, if I am going to have any effectiveness here, I am going to have to figure out how to be humble enough and ingratiating enough to be heard. But, not so much to be a complete doormat, and to be just disregarded as a toady of what their vision of Americans were.

"So, I was going to have to figure out how to deflect their criticism and their cultural expectations of an arrogant Yank to get things past the superficial stage and into some really cool, deeper, strategically better, pointed initiatives."

Miller had sorted through the overall aims for his communication. Over the next year, through many conversations and some research into the history of the Australian submarine force, he got his message on point. It paid off.

Gradually the relationship improved and peaked a year into his assignment. Miller was invited to speak at the annual mess dinner at HMAS Stirling, the Royal Navy base where the Australian submarine fleet is based in the west. He had to define communication objectives for his speech.

"My whole two years there, I was walking this tight rope between 'We have a lot of resources to bear, we have some great weapons, we have some great stuff', and then the

Australians have this inferiority complex, they call it the Tall Poppy syndrome. That's what they call it themselves. If you stick your head up above the other poppies, they will mow you down. So, they don't like anybody to take the lead and to be arrogant."

Miller had noticed that the Australians seemed to always be comparing themselves and thinking of themselves as in the shadow of the US when it came to their submarines. He wasn't seeing signs of the pride and esprit de corps he was used to in the US military. Maybe because displays of pride were seen as arrogance, he thought to himself.

"The thing is, the US submarine force mission is totally different than the Australian submarine force mission. Where they go, what they are trying to do, is different.

"And they have a great history. In World War I, the Australians used their AE2 submarine to do some stuff in the straights of Bosporus in the Gallipoli campaign. They did some good submarining. So, they have these things that serve as a thread of their tapestry, and they don't make a big deal of it."

Miller decided to do it for them. At the dinner, he told the AE2 story, but with a twist. "I told it from the perspective of a Yank," he grins. "How would a Yank have operated that submarine during that campaign?

"Totally satirical, totally with reverence to their history and their stuff. I got sort of all fired up and gung-ho, rah-

rah Australian submarine forces, and it was probably one of my happiest days that I spent there, because I worked hard to get this right, and they loved it."

Miller ended up briefing their minister of defense a couple of times, and he got a citation from their chief of navy, which none of his predecessors had. He attributes his success to the thinking and effort he put into honing his communication.

"I worked out how to try to get the message across without it getting stopped at the cultural gate."

Miller thought about how his Australian colleagues perceived themselves and those around them and crafted his communication accordingly. Understanding world view is a great way to get that inside perspective.

In some cases, the problem is slightly different. The cultural barrier may be more about the disparity in what people comprehend. Sometimes you need to tailor your message by thinking about what people might already know, and what they might not.

Marine Corps Master Sergeant Harry Dreany knew walking into that classroom in Afghanistan that he had his work cut out for him. He was tasked to train Afghan soldiers on how to detect improvised explosive devices (IEDs). That included teaching them to operate metal and mine detectors.

"We Marines have a lot of experience training other

Marines," he says. "But we're not really trained on how to train foreign nationals. We're just told to go train them. I expected that we couldn't necessarily follow the processes and procedures we usually use."

It was tough going. Every time Dreany walked into the classroom it was like he was hitting a replay button.

"Have you ever seen the movie *50 First Dates*? It was like we started from scratch almost every time," he says. "And I'm like, well, we talked about it last time. But it was like the words were lost in translation. I was getting a lot of blank stares."

"It was frustrating. We wanted these guys to go out and actually do patrols by themselves. But we weren't comfortable allowing them to do that if they couldn't retain the training. We'd just be sending them out basically to blow up and not do a good job."

To figure it out, he had to get inside their heads and see where they were coming from. Outside of class, Dreany went and talked to the interpreter he'd been assigned. It took a few go arounds with his interpreter and his colleagues before he tracked down the disconnect.

"They didn't understand the concept of an on/off switch," he says. "They just had never really experienced technology. So, they had a complete lack of understanding of just the basics. A simple on and off switch. Batteries. You know, you have to keep your batteries fresh in order for the system to work. Things like that were foreign to them."

He used these insights to make a better plan for communicating the lesson. Dreany had to change his starting point. He realized now that he couldn't just walk into class and say, "Fire up the system."

Instead, he built a checklist that started with "Take the device out of the box," and included every little step that was implicit in what it means to fire up a system—like locating the switch, turning the system on, testing the sensitivity, extending the mine receptor poles to the desired length, making sure the straps were adjusted correctly, and testing the batteries and the speakers.

"Without the checklist, they wouldn't even take it out of the box. They would just look at it," he says.

Another kind of situation that demands careful preparation is when your audience has little interest in even listening to you. This could be due to differences in perception of value or opportunity. A first step is to figure out their point of view. Then, find a way to describe the benefits of what you're trying to get across when planning your communication.

"It's like trying to convince a two-year-old to do something. Or anybody, for that matter," says retired Army Lieutenant Colonel Ike Merrill. "If there aren't any cookies there, they aren't going to do it."

Merrill was helping the Afghan Army set up an

intelligence school. The goal was to create an institution that was run entirely by Afghans, for Afghans. It would allow them to build and sustain their own capability. It was a great concept—with a major problem.

"The Afghans that were recruited to become instructors were completely unmotivated to train, to learn," Merrill says. "You know the acronym Retired on Active Duty? These guys were kind of like that. They were just putting in their time."

Puzzled, Merrill pulled out what he calls "the greatest interrogation tool of all time." Chai. He sat down with the instructors-in-training. They talked; and most importantly, he listened. He learned they were at the school because they had been told to be here, not because they wanted to be. "They all felt they were at the end of their careers and had been just sort of dumped there," he says.

He gathered from the conversation that these guys had been picked because they weren't involved in any ongoing operations, and they weren't critical to anyone's status. They were outside the circle of influence, and they had no influence of their own. So, they were just marking time.

It was clear to Merrill that the promise of doing their jobs better wasn't enough to motivate this group to participate. So, he tried to think about the situation from the Afghans' point of view. They weren't critical to anyone's status. They were outside the circle of influence.

Certainly, attending the intel school provided status for them, Merrill thought to himself. Why didn't these guys see that? How could he get that across to them?

Merrill thought back to the time when he had retired from active duty. He had to figure out what to do with his life and his career. He had sat down and listed all the skills he had as an intelligence officer. Then he mapped those skills to different careers. It seemed the same thing could be done here. So, that's what he did.

Merrill pulls out the spreadsheets he created and points. "If you go to the one that says *Driver-Interpreter/Translator*," he says as he moves his finger across the row. "The driver's skills. His skill is driving. He understands English, at least enough to know where to go."

"See, a driver can become an Interpreter/Translator, and then move all up the line: intel, command, leadership position, course research and development, attaché duty."

Merrill showed the student instructors how the skills they learned at the school could be used to advance their careers, and to improve their income. Their motivation increased tremendously.

"They looked at this and said, 'Oh, my gosh. Hey, we have all these opportunities,'" Merrill says with a gleam in his eye.

To think something new or do something different from what they're used to, people have to understand why it benefits them. That's what Merrill focused on. He identified the cookie. He figured out how the Afghan intel students could benefit personally. He found something of value to them they would gain from the training. They would increase their income and their position in their social circles of influence.

Stepping back and thinking about his strategy for communicating gave Merrill a way to gain momentum in getting the intel school off the ground.

Any time you walk into an encounter, you have an opportunity to inject thoughts that stick. Influence decisions in a way that makes a difference. To make it happen, you first have to take a step back. Think about your agenda ahead of time. Pin down what you want out of an interaction.

Then, work out how you're going to get it. Draw on what you know about the person, the context surrounding your interaction, and their culture. It might take some digging.

Think about the different ways you can communicate. The channels you have available. Shape your plan to the people and place. Then fire off your message.

Key Points

- Before diving into critical interactions, pause and think about what you really want to achieve

- Consider how to best express yourself and your messages to achieve your objectives

- Use your cultural knowledge to tune your transmission to the people you're dealing with

12

HOW TO ADAPT YOUR STYLE
AND STAY TRUE TO YOURSELF

"I'm about a foot taller than the average Indonesian," laughs Marine Corps Major Brewer. "I'm six four and in those days, I weighed about two hundred and ten pounds. So, I'm a big person. I'm bald and I'm African American."

Brewer is a Southeast Asia foreign area officer who couldn't look less like an Indonesian. When Brewer had an occasion to meet the local mayor in the area where he was assigned, he lowered himself. He didn't look the man directly in the eye. He didn't give him a firm handshake. He knew that an Indonesian wouldn't do those things. It was a way to show respect.

"Because of my appearance, a lot of foreigners, they don't expect me to take any of their cultural norms into account. When I turn around and participate in their customs, it really makes me stand out in a positive way," he explains. "When the bar is set so low, it's easy to clear it."

We are who we are. Tall, short, skinny, or bulky. Have

high-pitched voices or barytones. But no matter what you look like, you're in control of the impressions you make. Whether you look more like The Rock, Jack Black, or Steve Buscemi you can decide if you want to come off as intimidating or comforting. Inconsiderate or kind. Rude or respectful.

This is good. It means you have a tool at your hands. You can use the way you present yourself to influence your intercultural interactions. To send the messages you intend to. And, make sure people's take-aways about who you are, and the things you have to say are on point.

Brewer was aware that people have certain expectations about how he'll behave because of his appearance. He used this to his advantage. By adapting his posture, his eye gaze, and his handshake he showed respect, sure. But he did more than that. He also showed that he wasn't clueless. Quite the opposite.

Working in another culture can sometimes feel like staggering around in a hall of mirrors at a carnival. The ways people respond to you can seem so off the wall. So random. It can become easy to lose sight of the fact that you have some control of what people see and hear when you step on the scene. And that it doesn't require a momentous transformation on your part. Even a slight change in your posture, or a delicate shift in the words you use can speak volumes.

Take Marine Lieutenant Colonel David Rababy. Rababy did something as simple as shuffle his pronouns to cast himself in a different light and calm a massive crowd of agitated Iraqis.

"There was a riot situation about to happen," he explains. "There were several hundred, maybe even 1,000 people out in front of the Palestine Hotel in Baghdad, where all the reporters were staying. They were starting to press up against the Marines at the wire."

Rababy was ordered to go out there and stop the situation before it escalated, and somebody got hurt.

"I went out to that crowd with absolutely no idea of how I was going to do this," he recalls. "But, on the way out, I grabbed one of the megaphones that the PSYOP guys have and then I got on top of a vehicle. And, honestly, I had no idea what I was going to say because how do I diffuse this situation? How do I resolve it without it escalating?"

Knowing the language, Rababy started speaking to the crowd in Arabic. "And that, alone, just immediately, when they heard someone dressed in the American military uniform speaking their language, everybody got real quiet," he says.

He had their attention. But what to say? Rababy realized that he had assumed people were probably protesting because the electricity had been shut off. But maybe something else was going on. So, he asked the crowd why they had gathered and what they wanted.

"People started hollering from the crowd, 'where's my cousin?

"Saddam took him and I don't know where he is.'

And another person would yell, 'where's Saddam.'

Others asked about the electricity saying 'It's been off for a week or 10 days now and we have no electricity. How can we cook without electricity?'"

Rababy realized that people had been in the dark about a lot of things. They were looking for information. He started answering their questions as best he could. They began to cool down a bit. After a little while, though, they seemed to get impatient. The crowd started to spin up again as people were yelling their questions.

"I suddenly noticed an older lady near the wire," he says. "She looked to be like a grandmother, dressed in all black. Because the crowd was so rowdy, they were pushing her into the concertina wire, hurting her."

"So, I said to them, 'This is not right, this is not how we treat our elders.' I switched from saying *you*, to *we*. I said, 'This is not appropriate. Poor grandma here is being pushed into the wire, and she's going to be hurt. We need to give her some room.'"

By shifting his speech from *you*, to *we*, Rababy presented himself as one of them. This had immediate consequences.

"That seemed to have a real positive effect on not only

calming the crowd, but they recognized that I understood, culturally, the importance of elders, and calling this lady 'grandma,'—that was the word I used when I spoke to them—that seemed to really make them friendly toward me, and then they became less aggressive toward the Marines and more responsive to my requests."

People around you are reading you. The way you look, what you wear. What you say and how you carry yourself. They read into these things, whether you want them to or not. You can't really avoid it. But you can work with it to accomplish your goals. Sometimes maybe what you want to do is display your authority. Other times, you want to show that you can be warm, that you care. Whatever your intent, you have to be deliberate.

When you're working in other cultures, it can be easy for signals to get crossed. This means it's especially important that the way you present yourself isn't just an expression of how you feel in the moment. You have to present yourself in a way that achieves the effects that move you toward your objectives.

This can sometimes mean making a change, adopting a style, or making a move you wouldn't usually have considered. Like Army Lieutenant Colonel Jim Dunn had to do in South Asia. A cyclone had hit the southeastern coast of Bangladesh and killed nearly 135,000 people. Dunn had spent the last three days on a reconnaissance mission to see how bad the damage was.

He was standing on the runway in uniform, dirty, sweaty, and tired. It seemed mindboggling that just days earlier this same runway had been covered in nine feet of water. As Dunn took in the destruction, a man sidled up next to him.

He then looked at Dunn with genuine curiosity and asked, "Who made you?" The man smiled and nodded eagerly, waiting for Dunn's reply.

In that moment Dunn realized that this man was the Bangladeshi Air Force sergeant major he had been waiting for—the flight-line supervisor monitoring the arrival of his helo. He cursed silently under his breath. He just wanted to get on board that helicopter. Go back to the capitol to shower, shave. Most of all snooze. A discussion about the origins of life? That was not at the top of his agenda.

Dunn's thoughts raced as fast as they could on inadequate sleep. "I'm thinking, OK, who made me?" He describes how somehow his mind zeroed in on a memory of the nuns who taught him from the Baltimore Catechism book when he was a kid.

"'Well, God made me,' I said to him. The guy gave me this huge smile and said, 'Yes! Yes! God made you and he made me.' And we stood there and hugged each other. It was completely unexpected."

"I am not an overtly religious person," Dunn continues.

"But it got him on my side. It got me in a helicopter and got me headed where I needed to be, and I wasn't being fake or anything. I was just trying to figure out where this ball was coming from and to return it to him. And it worked really well."

Sometimes being disciplined about how you present yourself means showing deference and respect. Returning the ball to people the way you think they hope or expect to have it returned. In some situations, you can get where you need to go by coming off in a way that communicates peaceable, accommodating intentions. But that isn't always the case. Occasionally, circumstances call for a show of strength and authority. To achieve your aims, sometimes you have to break with people's expectations and even be impolite.

Colonel John Haseman was the defense attaché at the American embassy in Burma. "I was on the way to work the day the Burmese military opened fire on unarmed demonstrators," he says.

Suddenly, as Haseman's driver was making his way through the gentle early morning traffic, the embassy administrative consul got on the little car radio system used by embassy staff. He was frantic. The Burmese army was shooting at a bunch of civilians on the street. The consul was suddenly caught in a mob.

Haseman quickly diverted his driver to make his way to

the scene. It was chaos. There were bodies in the street and people running away. The consul's car was in the middle of the crowd. Stuck. Taking fire.

Haseman's driver pulled the car up so close to the action that the Burmese soldiers took notice. Surprised, they stopped firing.

Then Haseman talked the consul through the next steps. "I got back on the radio and said, 'OK. Get down on the floor in the front seat and you'll be OK because the engine will stop the bullets," Haseman says.

"I jumped out of the car and immediately spotted a young Burmese officer. I went over and identified myself as an American attaché, as a colonel, and showed him my ID card and I said, 'You're shooting at an American diplomat and I want you to stop immediately.'"

The argument quickly got heated. The Burmese officer thought Haseman was interfering with their security requirements—that he was objecting to their management of the mob.

So, he told the officer, "No I'm not. I'm interfering because you were shooting at an American diplomat. You've got to stop shooting at him and let him get out of there."

The whole conversation took place in English, even though Haseman did speak some Burmese. "I wanted to use my language, but I didn't remember getting a template for this dialogue from class," he says with a grin.

Haseman and the officer were going back and forth when suddenly he heard one of the soldiers say in Burmese, "We could shoot this man and claim it was an accident."

Although shocked and enraged on the inside, Haseman didn't let it show. "I immediately used an authoritative figure and body language by leaning against the front of my car with my arms crossed. Which, this is a no-no."

He explains that in many Asian countries crossing your arms is seen as rude. It makes you look like you're better than the person you're talking to. "I was being authoritative and rude on purpose to get his attention," Haseman says.

Shortly after, he heard the consul on the car radio. Haseman's intrusion had interrupted the shooting, and the consul had taken advantage of the break. His car was out of the crowd. With that, Haseman made an exit as well.

Putting the proverbial foot down—sometimes you have to do it. In high intensity situations you may need to draw lines in the sand and take a tough stand. More often than not, though, it can be to your advantage to survey your options. You might be able to achieve the same effects with a softer approach. Not necessarily ones that require you to humble yourself. But ones that get you results through subtler forms of power.

Picture this: You've been assigned as an advisor to a commander of an Afghan National Army battalion. After meeting with the commander briefly in private, he shows you to a large room. Here you're about to meet the rest of the battalion leadership and staff for the first time. This introductory meeting officially marks the replacement of your predecessor and the Army National Guard team who have been working with the unit prior.

About a dozen Afghan officers are scattered about the room, some sitting and some standing. One at a time they each introduce themselves, make a few comments and praise Allah. Your interpreter whispers each of their comments into your ear.

They make it around the room to a man who the interpreter tells you is the unit's religious officer. This officer stands up and like the others first says, "Praise be to Allah." Then he points his finger directly at you and exclaims, "This man is a jerk."

The comment reverberates through the room. Everyone turns their gaze to you. Silence. What runs through your head? What do you do?

This actually happened to Marine Corps Lieutenant Colonel Mike Carter only a few days after he landed in Afghanistan. Carter was surprised and taken aback. Annoyance hit him fiercely and fast.

"My first thoughts were, 'Here I am, leaving my family behind, I don't need to take this crap,'" he recalls. "I wanted to say, 'Hey, buckaroo, I'm here to help you guys, you're not doing anything for me here.'"

But he didn't say that. Carter did his best to hide what was running through his head. Because he knew that showing his annoyance would do little to further his mission. He was able to set his anger and disappointment aside by focusing on what he was there to accomplish.

"I knew that in order to be effective I could never show that I had lost my temper," he says. "I had to remain calm, cool, and collected."

First impressions were at stake. Carter knew that his ability to be respected as a level-headed, credible professional, to be someone whose advice the Afghans would have reason to take seriously, hinged on what he did next.

"If I was perceived by the Afghans in that moment to come unglued, they would probably think that I couldn't control my emotions," he explains. "I wanted to show them that not only could I remain cool but that I could turn the situation around and be in control. I thought the best way to do that was to try to be humorous. Without looking crazy, of course," he says with a smile in his voice.

He stood there in the room full of Afghans, momentarily stoic. Then, he cracked a little grin and said, "Clearly you are a very wise man, my friend. For my wife, too, thinks I'm a jerk."

The room was silent for an agonizing few seconds. Then the Afghans broke out in a cacophony of laughter.

In hindsight, Carter thinks that the officer might have been trying to test him to see how he would react to the insult. Perhaps the unit had had a negative experience with the US team that was there prior. He also thought it was possible that it was a personal power move. He might have been trying to show Carter that he was the voice of the battalion as the religious officer.

A while after the initial meeting, Carter circled back and discussed the incident with him. The officer was guarded about the reasons for his behavior. Carter decided not to push the issue beyond what was necessary. But the officer did seem to appreciate that Carter had sought him out. The two went on to develop a good relationship. In fact, Carter ended up considering the religious officer as his biggest advocate through the deployment.

Carter's ability to keep his reactions in check had been seriously challenged. But he was successful because he was able to set his emotions aside and draw a line between what he felt and what he was there to do, and then present himself in the best way to achieve his goals.

It might be starting to feel like being in control of the way you present yourself is all about putting on a show. Kind of like acting in a movie or a play. It isn't. Being deliberate about how you display yourself is not about being false. It's not about giving people the impression that you're someone you're not. For one, keeping that up would be massively exhausting. Also, it doesn't really work.

People may look very different from you. Say, they sport a turban, a lip plate, or a face tattoo. Or they might think and act vastly different from you. Don't let that fool you into thinking they'll miss it if you're insincere.

As Master Chief Petty Officer Dale Carter puts it, "You've got to drop the armor. You've got to show a real interest and be sincere. Because if you're not sincere, they pick up on that instantly, and basically, you make it worse because they think you're just after something. Or you're somebody who you're not. So, you have to be a real person."

Being genuine and being real. This can mean displaying the true parts of your personality, beliefs, and natural way of being that can help you be effective where you're working.

"One of the things we were told was 'Do not engage the Iraqis in conversations about Christianity. Do not talk religion with them,'" says Marine Corps Lieutenant Colonel Jamison.

"Well, when I got over there, it was getting close to Christmastime and the Iraqis would want to engage me on Christianity. They wanted to understand the Christian holiday. They would talk to me about my own Christian beliefs, and, they wanted to engage me on what I thought and knew about their belief system. Because that was important to them."

So, Jamison engaged them, and he didn't shy away from telling them what he believed. He made sure to show that he respected their beliefs, and with a few select individuals, he decided he could take the conversation to the next level.

One of his interpreters made a statement. "He said, 'Well, in my faith we think Jesus was a great prophet.'"

Jamison eyed the opportunity to have a real exchange and retorted, "I don't understand how you can." The interpreter was flabbergasted, his eyes big, trying to understand what Jamison was saying.

"In your faith," Jamison explained, citing an argument he'd read by C.S. Lewis, "if you don't believe Jesus was the Son of God, then you can't say he was a good prophet because he professed to be the Son of God. So, he is one or the other. Either Christ was the Son of God or he was a liar."

Jamison didn't have this kind of provocative conversation with all the Iraqis who wanted to talk about religion. Only some. Ones he thought would appreciate the dialogue. And he never found himself in a shouting match. The response was always positive.

"I think the reaction was good because they appreciated that I had awareness and tolerance for their beliefs, and they came to understand that I would tell them up front what I thought. Not in a confrontational way, but in a solid belief way."

To Jamison this honesty was key to developing meaningful relationships. "Regardless of culture," he says, "If you are not speaking frankly with me, if we can't have a conversation and develop some common ground, then why would I want to establish a relationship?"

Managing your self-presentation means highlighting some aspects of your natural self, and downplaying others. Take a look at yourself. Think about the aspects of yourself you want to share. The aspects that can help you make the impressions and send the messages that further your objectives. Accentuate those.

On the flipside, keep an eye on your characteristics that might hurt your cause. Say your usual manner of talking comes off as aggressive in the area you're working, or you just can't find tactful ways to share your true beliefs. Make an effort to keep those bits in check.

Marine Corps Master Sergeant Waters had to find a way to walk that line. "I think taking one extreme or another is maybe too much. I think you have to know what your limitations are in the culture and what's acceptable, or not, and things that are about you and your personality that you may need to put aside for a while. Just kind of put them in the background of your mind so they're not at the forefront.

"Say maybe you're a really loud talker, and that's how you are and how you usually connect with people because you're just very vibrant, and maybe the culture is calm, and they talk really slow and it's like going down to the southern part of the United States. In most cases you have to find an approach that's somewhere in the middle."

You have to find ways to be really truly genuine, otherwise people will write you off and tune you out. You also can't just script your performances in advance. You have to pay attention to the way people react, to read how they respond to you and be ready to adjust and switch up your game. Because self-presentation strategies that work in one place or situation don't necessarily work in the next.

Major Moreau is an Army foreign area officer. While she worked at the American embassy in Jordan, she also taught English at a local university.

"When I was teaching in Jordan, I wore a scarf. I completely covered up. I didn't have to, but it made the students and the officers more comfortable, because I was the only woman in the whole school. So, it's just so I didn't stand out for them."

Meanwhile, Marine Corps Master Sergeant Waters didn't find the headscarf useful at all in Afghanistan.

"I brought one with me because I read, 'Oh, bring one, you always want to have one on because you're a female.' Plus, I have really red hair, so I do stick out," she laughs.

But it didn't have the effect she'd hoped. "The day I went in and interacted with the men they started calling me their little sister. I'm like, there's no way," she says.

With the men, Waters found that the headscarf put her at a disadvantage when it came to respect and credibility. The headscarf didn't have the intended effect with the women either. But for a different reason.

"On one hand, they thought it was funny. It was like I was dressing up. On the other, they would tell me, 'You're American and you're going to be like me? We don't even like wearing it half the time.'" The women told Waters, "We do it because of fear. It's like our protection. It's like we have to. But then here you are. You try to be like us and we're trying to get out from under this."

Waters hadn't anticipated the effect wearing the headscarf could have—that for these women, it could make it seem she was in a way undermining their struggle to change their situation. So, she stopped wearing it.

The headscarf works in some situations and not others. It's the same with facial hair. Sometimes there's an advantage to bearding up. Sometimes there's not. It all depends on where you're going, who you're working with, and what you're doing. So, you have to feel out your approach and decide what works best on a case by case basis.

Sometimes you'll find that all you have to do is make a small adaptation, like changing what you wear or adjusting how you phrase something. Other times you might want to switch up something momentous. Like your entire living situation.

When Lieutenant Colonel Russell Jamison arrived in Iraq, he was met by an Iraqi army unit that had not been shown much respect by their predecessors. That was their perception, and as a result, they were icy and uncooperative. Jamison had to mend relationships. He thought about how the Iraqis viewed him to figure out how to present himself.

"I decided that we would take our meals with the Iraqis. We would not go to the American chow hall. We would spend time and that we would live in the same building as our Iraqi counterparts," Jamison says.

He explains that this allowed the Iraqis to see Jamison and his team not just in staff meetings, but also on the way to the head. "Not to gross anybody out, but they were seeing us going through our humanity. What is the adage? They saw us putting our trousers on one leg at a time." And in the course of that the Iraqis opened up a little bit more.

Carter, Waters, and Jamison changed what they wore, said, and did deliberately. Adapting and adjusting your behavior and the way you present yourself can be a great strategy to achieve certain impressions in the people you work with. You're not bending, stretching, or changing yourself just to be accommodating. You're doing it to get your job done.

Marine Master Sergeant Waters thinks about it this way.

"In this dynamic security environment, where you go in somewhere and you're the guy who is not going to be there for very long, you have to find a way to make yourself the best that you can be to make the impact that your commander wants you to have."

To do that, you have to be mindful of how well the messages you convey line up with what you're trying to achieve, because it's inevitable that some changes to your business as usual will need to be made.

Be on the lookout for alternative ways to get your points across. Find new ways to meet people's expectations, manage their impressions, and blow through their stereotypes when you need to.

As Major General Bell puts it, "You have to adapt how you are speaking—fit in and adapt how you are presenting yourself wherever you are in the world. Every culture or organizational culture I've ever been in, you have to do that if you want to be successful.

"The way you speak and hold yourself depends on your location, as well as how well you know the people you are with. But a little diplomacy and tact is always useful."

Key Points

- The way you present yourself has an influence on intercultural interactions

- Adapt your style within reason to achieve your aims in the culture and situation

- Tune in to how you are coming off to cultural others and adjust as needed

13

BACK TO YOUR MISSION

"In the Horn of Africa, lots of people use khat," says Major General Bell. Khat is a leafy plant that people chew to get a buzz. It's a narcotic. It's a controlled substance in the US and many other places in the world. But not in Somalia.

"Whenever there's a gathering, groups of men will sit around and chew khat, and much like wine snobs in other parts of the world, they will be khat snobs, talking about all the different kinds of khat, what makes some good or better than other khat," says Bell.

Bell could have taken a hard line on khat during his tenure there and lectured about the problems of drugs or the virtues of a drug-free culture. But turning the culture away from khat was not in the mission scope. He took a different tack that better served his aims.

"I learned what I could about khat, so I could talk about it with them, and I would ask the men questions about it and have them explain different aspects. It's a common topic, and noncontroversial. It would help to get them talking, open up to me, and help me build relationships."

"Americans are not good at understanding the importance of relationships. Once you have those, people will do things for you that they wouldn't otherwise."

While Bell was in the Horn, a young Marine in his command took a different stance toward khat. He searched an airplane that turned out to be loaded with the intoxicating plant.

"He pulled it out to the middle of the runway and burned it," Bell says. "The knucklehead. That caused us lots of trouble. It was unnecessary and outside his mission. If it doesn't cause a problem for the mission, it's not a problem you have to act on."

Sometimes, you have to separate your personal values from what you're there to do. Your role might be to build military capability and tighten partnerships, give a boost to a fledgling political system, improve infrastructure, or provide inoculation against extremism. It's your job to make sure things are different when you leave. Yet, even though you're there to stimulate change, you're not there to make them Americans. So, how do you set boundaries?

"In terms of where to draw the line, I would say that you don't have to compromise your moral values, but you do need to withhold your judgment," says Bell. "Like when people would offer me khat. I'd say, 'No thanks, I'm not allowed to do that. But I hope you have a good time.'"

Naturally, that doesn't mean you always tiptoe around the people you're working with, that you never step in and act. It's more about being clear about your specific purpose in the region and how that may align or differ with your general feelings about doing good. It's about keeping within the limits of your mission.

"We had a policy that no technicals were allowed outside specific areas," says General Bell. A technical is a big truck with a weapons mount. He pauses a moment. "Well, we found one outside the limits."

Bell was escorting a band of local leaders when he spotted the vehicle. "It was embarrassing. I had to make a detour with these folks in tow, and go stop the truck," Bell reminisces. "We pulled it over, and it was loaded with khat."

This put the group in a pickle. To resolve it, Bell had to walk on the razor's edge.

"We seized the truck and sent it back to base," Bell says. "The African who was driving, we put out on the side of the road. Along with his khat. We explained the security situation to the driver and locals who were with us, but didn't do anything with the khat. The locals all seemed relieved."

At times you will face a tough decision. Do you go along with local cultural practices—accommodate and give people the responses and solutions they want and expect?

Or do you push back, step in and intervene, even if it means cutting against the cultural grain? Unfortunately, the answer is not always simple. It depends on the situation. Yet you do have one dependable compass. Your mission.

Consider what happened when Major Moreau received a bizarre request in Jordan. Moreau is an Army foreign area officer. While she worked at the American embassy in Jordan, a US Special Forces team came over to train Jordanian forces. She was assigned to observe and coordinate. When it came time for the final evaluation of their urban house-clearing skills, the US instructors rigged a building with traps and different obstacles. The Jordanians' task was to go in and secure it.

The day before the exercise, the Jordanian commander made an unexpected request. "They wanted the answers before they went in," Moreau says. "They wanted to know where the booby traps were. We can't give you that! You have been trained. It's supposed to be a surprise to you. We want to see how you can react. In real life, you are not going to have the answers, you just go in."

Moreau explained the rationale to the commander for keeping the exercise blind. "I said, 'That is part of the training. If you fail, then we can see the mistakes and then you can train better.'"

A back and forth ensued. But the Jordanians wouldn't budge. "'We're not doing it,' they said. 'Our leadership will be there to watch this, and we don't want to send our people in to secure this building and look like fools because they failed.'"

There was no way around it. The Jordanians refused to participate unless they were given the plan ahead of time.

Moreau took the issue to the US team. They all stepped back and analyzed the situation. Their objective was to conduct joint training with the Jordanians to enhance interoperability. The Special Forces team who had been working with the Jordanians attested that the guys had been performing effectively and were in fact well-trained. There really was no reason to expect that they wouldn't complete the exercise successfully.

"So, we did end up giving them the answer sheets," says Moreau.

The Jordanians didn't want to take a risk in front of their higher-ups, and the Americans wanted to wrap it up. "If they were not well-trained, it would have been different. But it made them happy, and it achieved our mission," she says.

When it feels wrong to go along with cultural practices that rub you the wrong way, ask yourself if it truly detracts from your mission objectives or not. Otherwise, you risk seeing challenges and obstacles you think you have to deal with that aren't really there. You risk setting objectives for yourself that are unrealistic and unnecessary.

But, what about that other type of situation? What do you do when going along with the culture goes against your mission?

Sometimes local beliefs and practices compromise your mission. In those situations, you can't just play along. You do have to push back. That can mean telling people things you know they don't want to hear. You know you risk coming off rude and disrespectful if you break with expectations. But sometimes it may be the best way to accomplish your immediate goals in an interaction or to achieve your long-term mission objectives.

Air Force Major Frank Lusher is a combat pilot. Over the years he has developed the personality and work style needed to function in the fast-paced, miniscule-margin-for-error environment that is combat flying. As he describes it, flying fighter jets for the US Air Force means being part of an "eat your own" culture.

To Lusher, being part of this organizational culture means routinely and publicly calling out your own and other's mistakes, both during flights and in lengthy debriefs. This, he says, is an essential part of a pilot and a flying team's learning process.

"If I am doing something dumb, dangerous, or different, I want you to speak up right away," he says, clarifying that "if you can't admit your mistake you will never get better. Plus, it can be dangerous."

While in Korea he was part of a number of joint exercises with the Koreans and Japanese, planning and flying joint missions. His role in the exercises was to help the Koreans and Japanese shape their air forces by consulting to develop their planning process. He found that Korean and Japanese partners were very hesitant to speak up, and this made it difficult to work with them.

He understood that within both cultures people have a great deal of respect for their elders and are very rank-conscious. He also understood the concept of preserving face and what this meant. At the same time, he saw these cultural values as sometimes going directly against the culture of learning from errors that needs to be in place in order to develop an organization that can execute combat flight operations successfully.

This became particularly clear to him after a big joint exercise. He found himself caught between a rock and a hard place. He had to choose between working within the culture or encouraging the style of interaction that in his experience leads to mission success.

"We were running a big training exercise and doing back to back air-to-ground and air-to-air debriefs," he recounts.

Everyone was gathered in an auditorium. They were watching the exercise play out on a big screen. The Mig1 (red side) was running the debrief. They were doing shot validation. This is an air-to-air replay where people talk through the shots they took and determine the outcome of each shot.

Lusher knew that one of the Japanese F15 pilots had a fratricide during the exercise and it got to the part where the pilot would talk through the shot. On the screen, everyone saw the pilot call out the target, verify the target a second time, and shoot.

As the pilot was talking through the verification part, right before he took the shot, Lusher saw his higher-level officer tap him on the shoulder, cutting him off, telling him to pretend it didn't happen. It passed by on the screen without a word.

"I waited until the guy running the debrief finished. He asked me if I had anything to add and I said, 'Oh, yeah.' I called it out right there in front of everybody. I said 'You took the shot. You had a frat. Just fess up to it and then go out and buy a keg and make it up to everyone here.' I wasn't going to let them cover it up."

In this situation Lusher deliberately went against expectations because he was there to change the organizational culture. The objective he had been given was to help shape Korean and Japanese combat flight operations. In his view, that meant encouraging open discussion of mistakes in the debrief.

Lusher was aware of the cultural expectations, and he knowingly made the decision to go against them. He knew what would happen if he called the pilot out, and he knew what would happen if he went along and pretended it never happened. He deliberately chose between these options.

Afterward, he followed up offline and explained to the Japanese why he did what he did. During his consultation, he showed the American approach to combat flight operations. In the end, the Japanese will ultimately decide how they accommodate or adapt that aspect within their own organizational process.

Even if circumstances require that you push against current norms and practices, it's often possible to find ways to show that you respect people and their culture. You can do that by showing that you understand you're running contrary to the natural cultural order.

Another way to manage culture-mission conflicts is to look for a third way forward. What if you could come up with courses of action that meet your objectives and accommodate the culture at the same time? Win-wins are always the most popular solutions all around, because everybody benefits. Sometimes it just requires a dash of out-of-the-box thinking.

In his nineteen years in the Marines, Major Wilson has forwarded around the world. Iraq and Afghanistan, of course. But also many locations in the South China Sea: Malaysia, Brunei, Indonesia, and Thailand, and in East Africa: Eritrea, Ethiopia, and Kenya.

Working as an advisor to the presidential guard in the United Arab Emirates was memorable for Wilson. Especially when he had to teach the president's men how to ski.

"Their commanding general wanted them to get well-rounded training. They are Special Forces guys. They need to be able to operate anyplace," Wilson explains.

He first took them to this ski club inside a Dubai mall. But there he discovered that the guys were taking turns to go into the restaurant to warm up. He needed them to experience doing this outside, to get a real feel for the conditions and the climate, so they could grow some hair on their chests.

So, he took them to Lake Tahoe in Northern California. The twenty-five Arab soldiers had never been in a mountainous environment, and they had never seen real snow.

"Yeah, they never saw snow in the UAE. Let alone how to operate in it and ski in it. So, the challenges there were numerous," says Wilson. It turned out the younger guys got into the skiing. They wanted to keep going because they were enjoying it, and because it kept them warm.

Not surprisingly, the cold was not something they enjoyed. But the way they dealt with it was a bit of a surprise to Wilson.

"I've seen five Marines squeeze into a four-man tent before," he says with wonder, "but never ten. They were stacked body upon body inside their tents. It looked like a Twister game."

The Arab soldiers had an even harder time getting used to the no-smoking policy in the park. But it was on the books and it was strictly enforced because of the fire hazard. Wilson told them they could use chewing tobacco instead. It's what the US guys used. But that was a no go.

"It was like smoking was important to them culturally, and when we told them they couldn't, they felt like their culture was being repressed a little bit."

A number of the UAE soldiers were hardcore smokers and they refused to quit. Wilson caught them over and over.

"I had to start pulling a lot of cigarettes out of their mouths and stomping them out. It put me in a very awkward position. I know I burned some bridges," Wilson says.

It became such an issue that the base commander said they'd have to kick them off base if they caught one more guy doing it. This would not look good for the strategic relationship.

He knew using force was a stopgap measure. He had to find a different way. The groundbreaking moment came when he suddenly had an insight.

He asked himself, "Why is smoking not allowed in the park? What is the root cause?" It was a fire hazard. Because of the flame. If there was no flame, there'd be no fire.

"I got permission to use electronic cigarettes," Wilson says with a hint of satisfaction. "The point was that they couldn't set fire to the forest. It wasn't that they couldn't smoke." The Arab soldiers were excited about them. They didn't have them in the UAE, so they were a novelty.

Wilson's primary objective was to maintain a good relationship with UAE leadership. To do that he had to make sure the Arab soldiers didn't go home feeling slighted or insulted, and this meant not getting kicked off the base.

The next group of Marines ended up really benefiting from the e-cigarettes, as well. They were bringing a group of 150 Arab soldiers into the park and would have had a much bigger problem.

How did he come up with a solution? He thought about the why. Why did people want things a certain way? What was the purpose of their rules? Their demands? What were their real objectives? The Arab soldiers didn't just want the nicotine. They wanted to smoke cigarettes. The base commander wasn't antismoking. He just didn't want a forest fire.

Sometimes you can find a win-win solution. A compromise. Others though, there's just no way around it. To achieve the ends, you have to risk coming off as rude and disrespectful. You'll run into situations where you can't accommodate people's needs, wants, and expectations and accomplish your goals at the same time. Even in those situations, understanding the culture can give you an advantage, such as helping you find the most effective way to drive your point home.

Marine Corps Lieutenant Colonel Page was at his wits' end. He desperately needed to convince an Iraqi man to get his family out of a huge hole full of volatile weapons crates before they, and everyone around the hole, were blown to high heaven.

Page and his unit had been working in an eastern suburb of Baghdad. On this particular day, on the way back from a recon, Page and his team had spotted thirty or forty Iraqi civilians coming up the road toward them. All of them were carrying wooden ammunitions crates.

"That was obviously something we needed to go investigate," Page says.

The team made their way to where the people were coming from. There, in the middle of a farm field, was a big hole.

"It was about the size of a two-car garage," Page remembers. The Iraqi military had dug a hole and dumped tens of thousands of rounds of 57mm antiaircraft ammunition in it.

"These things are extremely large bullets, and they have a big primer in the back. If that was struck, then the bullet would go off and a chain reaction would explode all the rest of them," Page explains.

Page secured the pit. As they were leaving, he glanced down the road. Through the farm field he saw a man's head sticking out of the ground. The man was clearly trying to hide. So, Page took a small team of three with him to investigate.

Deeper into the field was another pit, same as the last one. In it was a man Page recognized as the leader of the local village with his wife and five kids. The little group had hauled twenty or thirty crates out already, and they were still digging.

Page tried to get the man to understand that he was in grave danger, that his family was in danger. His Arabic was pretty poor at the time, but using his phrasebook he was able to convince the man that it was unsafe.

"After a long back and forth he finally motioned his two sons to come out of the pit," Page says, "leaving his wife and three daughters working in there. He was trying to get me to understand that it was up to God whether the pit exploded or not."

At this point Page realized that he was wedged between a rock and a hard place. He had stressed safety, and the man had actually responded—in his own terms.

"The fact was that it wasn't a big deal if his wife and daughters were killed. I knew the cultural difference in how we operate was pretty serious. But I didn't want to have to give up and leave them there."

One of Page's Marines was a female lieutenant. He called her over next to him and asked her to remove her helmet.

"She had her hair done up on her head, but he could obviously see that it was a woman. And then I explained to him that she was not only a woman but a Marine. An officer, no less."

Page immediately got the reaction he was looking for. The man was visibly startled.

"And then I explained to him that she was upset that he wasn't listening to me. And I told her to try to look mean, so she was standing there, kind of grimacing."

Page looked the man in the eyes, pointed at the female lieutenant, and laid it out. If he didn't get his family out of the pit and move on? She was going to shoot him.

"He physically moved back. Brought his hands up in front of him and started saying, no, no, no," Page describes.

"You would never have a woman carrying a gun as an officer in a military unit in Iraq. All of that tied together was enough to intimidate him, I think. To the point where he believed that she would actually shoot him."

Page asked the man one more time to take his family and leave. He finally agreed and waved at his family and motioned them to follow him.

Page never wanted to actually get physical. "We were never going to go there. Of course. No one was going to really shoot him," he stresses.

But Page considered the man's point of view and recognized that he couldn't just leave. Not without putting up some resistance. If he did, he would be shamed, and he needed to maintain his social reputation.

"But I needed to pull him off his game, get inside his decision cycle," Page explains.

And he did that by taking the man's perspective. He understood how females are viewed by Iraqi men and knew that being shot by a woman would be an embarrassment—much worse than being shot by another man.

"I understood his view of women was something that I could take advantage of. By bringing a woman into the mix, I changed the rules," he says.

Page used this understanding of the culture to come up with a way to make an impression that would convince the man to stop endangering his family. Instead of himself, he put a female Marine at the front of the interaction to send a signal.

In this case, Page had to go against the culture. He couldn't just leave the female members of the family in the hole, even though the family's patriarch believed that their survival was up to God. Letting them go about their business conflicted with his mission to maintain security in the area.

Sometimes local beliefs and practices compromise your

mission. In those situations, you can't just play along, and that can mean telling people things they don't want to hear. But, even in those situations, knowing a little about the culture can help you be effective and minimize damage.

Sometimes it can feel like you're stuck between two bad options. Do things their way or accomplish your mission. Accept things that don't make sense—things you don't approve of—or risk pissing people off.

The things people from other cultures say, think, and do can at times feel like a bitter pill to swallow. Yet, sometimes accepting it is the best way to go. If their behaviors or practices don't compromise your mission, going along may be the best way to build and maintain relationships. Relationships you need to achieve your main purpose for being there.

Making this switch in your thinking can be tough, because you get invested. You spend months and years of your life trying to make a difference and you want to be successful. When you see things that don't meet US standards, and people continue to behave in ways that seem wrong, it can feel like you're getting nowhere.

Anticipate that your sensitivities and standards will be insulted and head it off. Read a bit about the local norms. What's accepted? What's not? Familiarize yourself with the local laws. Are drugs legal? Prostitution? Carrying open alcohol containers in public? What activities are legal there you would never have considered and the other way around. Think about how your own background shapes the way you view these things.

Temper your expectations and put a leash on your opinions. Otherwise you make your job tougher than it already is.

"In Iraq, we came up the slogan, 'Iraqi good enough,'" says General Bell. "The idea was not to try to convert them to the exact US military ways, but instead to make them good enough to deal with their own challenges."

Understanding cultural differences doesn't always mean accepting them. You can't be accommodating in all situations. Use your mission as a guide. Do away with the ugly American, but don't replace him with a stooge.

Figure out where people are coming from culturally, so that when you act contrary to local norms, you do it in a thoughtful way.

Once you have a clearer view, you may be able to spot a different path from A to B. A path with less resistance, and one that works for everybody.

Key Points

- Keep an eye on the limits of your mission and avoid overstepping those boundaries

- Don't try to impose US customs and laws or make other cultures exactly like the US

- Manage conflicts between your mission objectives and local cultural norms

ABOUT THE AUTHORS

Drs. Louise Rasmussen and Winston Sieck are co-founders of Global Cognition. They aim to advance cultural competence in demanding environments through research, training, and assessment. Their scientific studies identified critical skills and strategies that enable people to adapt quickly to new cultures and work effectively with diverse partners. Drs. Rasmussen and Sieck have written for numerous scientific and trade publications, from the *Journal of Cross-Cultural Psychology to Military Review.*

To learn more or get in touch with the authors, visit www.globalcognition.org.

Made in United States
Orlando, FL
11 April 2022

16738764R00157